So, Why Not Me?

A Guide to Help Transform You Into Greatness

By Aja Waters

Printed in the United States of America First Printing, 2016
ISBN 978-0-692-69472-5
Queens See Queens LLC Philadelphia, PA
www.sowhynotmebook.com

This book is dedicated to my guardian angel, my beloved Grandmother, Delois Rhonda Stokes-Bell. (March 27, 1951-August 31, 2011)

You have taught me so much about being myself and accepting who I am. You fought so hard for my siblings and I to have a better life. I miss you more and more every day and I know you would be extremely proud of me.

You're vibrant, loving, transparency, and bold spirit will be missed. Thank you for your sacrifice, friendship, love, thoughtfulness, humor and memories.

I am thankful to be your granddaughter.

Love,

Aja

TABLE OF CONTENTS

ACKNOWLEDGEMENTS

I want to first and foremost thank my Father in heaven who has given me the vision, tenacity, and diligence to write this book. Without God, I am nothing and I am glad that our relationship is becoming stronger as I get older. I thank you for not giving up on me. There are so many people I want to thank, but I would like to highlight some key individuals who helped me during this time of writing my book.

Nehemiah Davis, you are simply amazing. You're the older brother I never had and I am honored to be a friend and mentee of yours. All you have ever been is helpful, genuine, and willing to help me become successful. You were the one who pushed me to write the book at this particular time in my life, and I could have not chosen a better time to get it done. May God continue to bless everything you touch and be prosperous in all that you do.

Next to my family, I love you and I will continue to make you all proud! To the members in my organization, Queens See Queens LLC, I want to send a huge thank you! Without you all, I wouldn't be able to do what I do- and that is to inspire. You ladies are awesome and I appreciate you all on different levels. I will continue to dedicate my work, and vision to the organization.

To all my mentors, whether it be close or from afar, you all have influenced me in many ways. I would like to thank Jim Rohn, Stephanie Cain, Kamilla-Collier Mullin, Pastor Rashiid Coleman, Marsha Corelien, Demetrius & Dhayany Walker, Bunmi Samuel and Lawrence Matthews. Thank you all for your wisdom and knowledge of business and life skills. Thank you to my editors and creative team: Jamillia Kamara , Kiarra Solomon, and "For His Glory Designs " LLC for collaboratively putting this book together. Writing my first book was definitely interesting, but you all made the journey worthwhile.

To Jaynay Chanel, who I met at a workshop not too long ago, you have been so helpful to my journey. Thank you for answering all of my questions and being supportive. That one conversation we had on the phone really helped me tremendously and I thank God we crossed paths.

To my mommy, Laurette Green Roberts, the relationship we have is unique and special. You've taught me tough love and how to have thick skin. My sassiness comes from you! I love you with all my heart and thank you for giving birth to a Queen.

THE INTRODUCTION

I was the girl in the audience imagining myself in the shoes of a speaker on the stage of a business conference in Las Vegas in the fall of 2014. She was a self-made millionaire, build an organization of over fifty thousand business partners, had her own clothing line, and Women's Empowerment Network.

She was a wife, a mother, and a true daughter of God. She was petite, with long chocolate brown hair and a presence that could light up an entire room. Her posture and energy introduced herself before she even spoke. I got so inspired by hearing her entrepreneurial journey, because I knew that God had transformed her into who she had become. To see a successful African-American woman speak to over two thousand people in an arena about her transition from employee to a self-made millionaire gave me hope.

From hearing her story, I became open to the possibility of achieving my very own dreams, and wanting more out of life. As I left the conference, I remembered hearing myself say, "So why not me? If this is what you want to do, then what are you waiting for?" The voice within became my "aha" moment, and for some reason that theme of "why not me?" keeps coming in every area of my life- even until this very day.

I left that conference feeling empowered and ready to take on the world, because at that moment I realized I wanted to spend my life educating and empowering others-especially women.

This is what I want for you- to receive your aha moment, and perhaps jumpstart the best years of your purpose-filled life. The concept of "why not me" identifies who you are and whose you are, while channeling that confidence into action. Before writing this book, I had several types of fears in my head: "I only have a high school diploma", "I never went to college", "I'm from West Philadelphia" "I'm a black female", and "No one will believe in me or buy this book"... blah, blah, excuses, excuses. Then after looking at those fac-tors, I had to ask myself, "Ok, and? What are you going to do now? Give up on writing this book? Or keep going anyway?"

Sometimes we have to blossom right where God has planted us, because that is what makes our stories unique. The mes-sage is the same. We all have heard stories about how people started from barely making it, regardless of race, age, sex, religion, education, etc. and still becoming a success story. Why? Because they believed that they could first. Either you can stay in the condition you are in, or fix it. There's nothing more powerful than a made up mind, and that's what I want for you- to make a decision to finally say, "You know what, why not me?", and take action! God made us all more than capable to do any and everything we put our minds to, the key is to believe that.

We all get to a point in our lives where we are ready to take a leap of faith, stretch ourselves, and get out of our comfort zone. However, whether it's taking on a new task, up for a new challenge, or looking for a new opportunity, we talk ourselves out of something that could be potentially great and miss out on them.

Later on we find ourselves seeing ordinary people making extraordinary moves and doing the things we were too afraid to do. We then question ourselves by saying, "That should've been me", followed by an excuse to why we didn't pursue it. So, why not you? Why can't you be happy, married, rich or living the life of your dreams? That's the purpose of why I created this book to help identify what has been holding you back from actually achieving the life you want.

While reading this book, I ask for your permission to allow me to be transparent with you, and for you to be open to receive the information from this book. I also ask that you take the information from this book and actually apply it, because it's not the knowledge or the value of this book that costs us in the long run- it's whether or not the knowledge is being applied that costs us. Take notes, enjoy and thank you from the bottom of my heart!

With Sincerity and Love,

Aja

“FIND OUT WHO
YOU ARE AND
DO IT
ON PURPOSE”

•••

Dolly Parton

Chapter One: Why Am I Here?

" The two most important days of your life are the day you are born and the day you find out why"
-Mark Twain

Why Am I Here?

At some point in our lives, we come to a point where we may ask ourselves this, "WHY I AM HERE?" Whether we are in a dead-in job full of stress, or looking at the ceiling of our bedrooms at night filled with anxiety, we all are subconsciously or consciously thinking about what our purpose is here on earth. Have you ever felt like you're not fulfilled or have told yourself, "There has got to be more to life than what I'm settling for?"

If this is true for you, it is likely that you're on the same boat like most of the world. Some of us tend to ignore finding out what our purpose is and go through life aimlessly without a mission or ultimate goal. We all have a purpose, job, function, or duty to fulfill in this lifetime. Whether you choose to recognize it or not, we all have something special about us and something to offer.

Although recognizing your purpose may appear to be difficult (because we live world that falsely showcases how everyone should look, talk, be, and act), once you suddenly notice it, life becomes more fulfilling and worth living.

Life isn't wrapped in the prettiest box, but it's still a gift, and it's important that we pay attention to why we are here. There's a quote that says, "If you're not living, then you're dying." Think about it. Every day is a day closer to your deadline here on earth and it would be sad that you leave this world unfulfilled and full of resentment.

I don't intend to be harsh in my last statement, but that's the reality and should be every reason to get up, and get going! Life isn't about just paying bills and dying, nor should it be a constant struggle- because you are meant to do more than just that. Your purpose is connected to energy, and energy is connected to everything.

This is what separates the inspired from the uninspired and determines if you live a life that's fulfilling or a life that's settling. My goal is not to tell you what your exact calling is; that's something you will find in your own self- discovery.

However, I can direct you or help spark the reason God chose you to be here- because it's there, and its waiting for you to see it and live in it. In this chapter, I want suggest a few concepts that could help guide you to answering the question of why you are here.

CLARITY

Clarity is so important to your journey. Once you have clarity about why you are here, you will unlock your purpose. In order to become successful, you must first have a clear vision on what it is you want from life.

It's not selfish to think in this manner at all! In fact, that's the way the world is supposed to be. We come from a universe that is abundant and is full of all the resources we need in order to live in our highest selves. The problem is, we have been taught since birth to live a safe, average and "lack thereof " type of lifestyle. This causes us to steer away from what our purpose really is- especially for individuals that may come from families with limited vision and resources, such as their environment, money, and education.

However, clarity is what can prevent all of those things from coming into existence. When you are clear of where you are going in life, you are more aware of the things that are not aligned to your purpose. Clarity is like having women intuition- no offense fellas. Just as women can have gut feelings about something or someone, likewise, clarity should bring that same gut feeling of knowing that you have purpose and the ability to shine bright. It's all a matter of becoming clear on who you are so that your faith and confidence surpasses your current reality.

Clarity simply means understanding, so the question is, where do you seek understanding?

About yourself, your life, your fears, your relationships or just in general? Understand that you alone cannot get clearness or direction- it has to come from a higher source of energy. Whether it be from God or whomever you seek spiritual guidance, tap into that source. It will significantly help during your journey of finding why you are here.

For me, prayer is my holy grail of understanding. Whenever I need clarity in any area of my life, I just simply pray! I believe prayer is having a conversation with God- which is where I receive energy and understanding from. Sometimes, I pray long and deep prayers. Sometimes my prayers are short and to the point! The solution I have for those who are looking to gain clarity as a way to navigate through life, is to simply connect with your spiritual teacher. You can only become clear about life through prayer, meditation and stillness.

There's a motivational speaker by the name of Les Brown- he has the ability to inspire like no other I remember watching a YouTube clip about a year ago on using motivation to get "unstuck" in life.

He used an example of a man who had it all: a wife, kids and a job, then one day lost it all. He was too ashamed to tell his family what happened so he left them to be on the streets-homeless. From my understanding, he became a beggar and met with a pastor to help him get his life back.

The pastor told him that he did not have the solutions to his problem and told the beggar to meet back with him once he found the answer to his problems. Angrily, the man left and did just that. The man went back to his vacant old building, where he lived, walked up and looked deep into a broken piece of a mirror that was left in the vacant space.

He look at himself in shame and guilt crying with tears down his face asking God, "What did I do to deserve this?". After a short moment of crying, suddenly he got back up, walked back to the mirror, and looked in awe-as if he saw a new man. As I continued to watch the YouTube clip, I said to myself, "Interesting!" The man first saw himself in a shameful manner, he prayed next, and then saw himself as a new man. Why was that? That moment between crying and feeling in awe, he became clear about his initial purpose in life. From that point of understanding, he was able to get back on his feet, and that's where Les Brown ended the story.

I believe Brown left viewers like myself with a cliffhanger, because the end result doesn't matter for the illustration at hand. What matters is that first step. The man became clear on who he was and knew that his set back did not define him or his purpose in life. I'm also pretty sure that the man in the story lived well after that point.

He mastered the first step of becoming clear own who he is and whose he is. Surely, if he had success before, he can obtain it again.

The same goes for anyone. Ultimately, clarity can aid you from facing failures or hardships and get you back on your feet. Getting clear on what your purpose is will make the journey simple, but not easy. Understand that clarity will not only help unlock your purpose, but it will also help you understand when trials and tribulations come your way. Clarity in a way, serves as the windshield wipers for your life; it prevents distractions that will try to blur out your purpose. Clarity appears when you are still, surrender, and kill all of the noise and distractions from around you and in you. Let me give you some pointers on how to get clear in your own journey.

HOW TO GAIN CLARITY

1. **Put God First:** God is the Creator of all things, tangible and intangible. Get clear on who He is and what He has planned for you. Allowing God to become first in your life puts you in position to receive all of the things God has to offer you.

2. **Be Exact On What You Want From Life:** The universe does not like confusion. Be clear on what you want out of life, so that you open the gateway for those things to attract to you.

3. **Pray, Meditate, & Be Still:** When you pray, you are asking. When you meditate, you are internally filtering out the bad and replacing with the good. When you are still, you are healing and allowing peace to be within you. These factors can enable you to obtain understanding in your journey and life.

With those three suggestions implemented, surely you will be on your way to achieving the first step of greatness! Using clarity to unlock your purpose will put you on the right track.

IDENTIFYING YOUR PURPOSE

Now that we understand the importance of gaining clarity, it is vital to know and identify your purpose. How do you identify what your purpose is? I believe signs of your purpose will appear once you set your mind to become ready to receive it.

There's a Zen Proverb that says, "When the pupil is ready, the master will appear". Once you are aware that you have purpose, the universe will show you exactly what you need to know. With that in mind, purpose is usually found where your passion lies. Ask yourself this, what are you passionate about? Is it helping people? Cooking? Singing? Creative Writing? Fitness & Nutrition? Think about that one thing you love to do. Now imagine yourself making that passion of yours into a living! Sounds crazy right? But get this, people are out there making a living and are loving what they do! Now it's time for you to get on the same page, so that you too can live a life you love!

Identifying your worth is not about what you're good at necessarily, but it is finding out what you're called to do. We can all learn a new skill, just like a dog can learn a new trick, but one rarely finds his or her purpose developing just skills.

The real goal is to learn skills and use those skills to enhance your calling! Steve Harvey once said on a segment of Oprah's show called "Life Class " that, "Your career is what you are paid for, and your calling is what you are made for."

I believe that's the best way to explain this point. Well said, Steve! I would even go beyond that statement by saying, "Your talents are what you are paid for, but your gift is what you are made for". Your calling is what God has given to you to help fulfill the works of the earth. Your gift is connected to your calling and your talents are connected to your skills. These skills can help you get into a career, obtain a promotion on a job, or to start a business. However, it's not connected to your purpose necessarily.

For example, I am really good at doing hair. That's a talent that I have; but, my gift is to inspire, consult and encourage others to see themselves better than they are. I get an indescribable feeling when I am inspiring someone to start a business or to go after his or her dreams. I get excited when I am speaking on entrepreneurship and personal development to an audience of women. On the other hand, I don't feel that way when I am doing hair.

Now this is not to say that doing hair is not a way of helping people because it is. Don't miss the point at hand. The goal is help identify your purpose, so how you choose to use your calling is what makes the difference.

Whether your dream or purpose is to become a beautician or start a business, make sure your heart and desire is in it. Remember this, talent is a doing process and your calling rather, is a feeling process which differentiates the two. You will know that you've recognized your purpose based on how it makes you feel. There is no better feeling than discovering your purpose and living in it.

HERE ARE 4 WAYS TO BREAK DOWN FINDING YOUR PURPOSE:

1. **Passion**: Ask yourself, what do you have a deep or strong passion for? Your purpose is usually found in where you passion lies.

2. **Experience**: They say experience is the best teacher, right? Experience is another way to find your purpose. Ex: *"Susan discovered her passion for teaching while tutoring at her local recreation center."* Experience gives you exposure and knowledge on what you like and dislike-which helps in finding your purpose.

3. **Become Omniscient In Your Life**: Being omniscient simply means to be "all-knowing" or to view something from a narrative standpoint. I learned this skill by reading a book called "The Power of Now" by Eckert Tolle. I learned that being present and aware of your thoughts can help identify your purpose. Spend time evaluating what works for you as opposed to what doesn't. Be aware of what you are naturally good at and work on it.

Become observant of the emotions that come with practicing this, then see if it can be turned into making a lifestyle for yourself.

4. **Use Prayer & Spiritual Guidance**: Everyone has a unique talent or gift that comes from God or a higher source. You may not be able to sing like Beyoncé or paint like Picasso, but you may have other talents that you can make a living from. Perhaps you can be really great at listening to people, or even can make a really good ham sandwich-which you can totally can make a living from both of these! If you are unsure of what your gifts are, ask the universe to reveal them to you. If God is where you seek understanding from ask God to help discover what your gifts are. Pray and ask. I promise you if you want to know badly enough, the universe will make sure that you will know.

WILL POWER VS. WHY POWER

Once you know the why behind the life you want, the how of getting there will come to past. This part is key to getting into unlocking your purpose. Without having a strong enough why, you'll never get to the how of achieving your life goals. Your "Why Power" must be stronger than your "Will Power". Why? Because it will be the "why" for whatever dream you are looking to accomplish that will determine the "how" to see it come to life. For instance, have you ever found yourself getting involved with something and quit as soon as it became too difficult or required too much of a commitment? If you have, it is because your why for it was not strong enough. That is why the diet, the business plan or any type of interest you may start fails because your why for it is weak. Let's use one of the most familiar topics, weight loss, to paint the picture of "Will Power" vs. "Why Power". Losing weight is probably number one on the "to do" list of New Year's resolutions for most people. Statistics say that the top three American New Year's Eve resolutions are to:

3. Spend less, and save more.
2. Get organized.
1. Lose weight.

The "Will Power" of losing weight is taking the necessary steps or actions to achieve your ideal weight. However, if your why is not coming from a position of desire, then you'll find every excuse to not drop the weight. This type of thinking will take you through another year feeling resentful or full of regret. Like most Americans, it's not just the weight that people are confusing both Will Power and Why Power. It's their entire lifestyle that's like the weight loss example. Remember, how you do anything is how you do everything. If you are having trouble in one area of your life, then most likely there are other areas in your life that aren't where they need to be. Trust me, I've been there in my own life and had to realize very quickly that all areas in life needs constant maintenance. Ultimately, the goal is to develop a strong enough why, so that the how will come eventually after it.

With that in mind, your why is connected to your heart, and your heart is the treasure chest for all of your desires. You become driven when your purpose and your why are in alignment with each other.

Your why is what gets you through the bumpy times of going into anything new or different, so that you are able to finish instead of giving up. Get in the habit of remind- ing yourself of your "why". Start asking yourself, "Why do I want to live a better life?" Once you can identify why the challenges exist in your current life, you can determine the how to simply fix them. Get into the habit of becoming aware of what's going on in your life. If you don't like it, fix it! That type of attitude will get you one step closer to change what's not working in your life and to focus on your purpose.

HOW TO IDENTIFY YOUR WHY POWER VS. WILL POWER

The chart below compares the differences between Why Power and Will Power:

WHY POWER	WILL POWER
• Why Power will drive you to keep going • Associated with reason or purpose • Why Power is mental	• Will Power will force you to keep going • Associated with action, requiring limited reasoning • Will Power is physical

See the difference? "Why Power" is internal and "Will Power" is external. The ultimate goal is to use both powers to help you achieve your life goals. Let your "Why Power" be eighty percent of your efforts and your "Will Power" be twenty percent of your efforts. If you can grasp that concept and make those powers come together, it will motivate you to keep going in your journey.

LISTEN TO YOUR FRUSTRATIONS & DISSATISFACTIONS

Knowing what the "why " is in your life will expose you to areas within it that may need tweaking. One of the ways to help alter those areas is to start paying attention to the parts in your life that you are dissatisfied with. We've been taught to believe that frustration is a bad thing, and that we should do everything possible to avoid it. Whether it's our jobs, relationships or weight, we pretend and act like the life we settle for doesn't bother us. We may tell ourselves, "Put on a fake smile, and suck it up", "Its ok. I'll just settle with this", and decide that misery is part of who we are. In reality, this could be the universe telling you that this is not what you you're supposed to be doing with your life.

Trust me when I say, that's not the jerk you're supposed to be dating, you shouldn't keep eating your emotions away, and your life isn't meant to be spent working behind a company's cubicle making minimum wage! Now- if you're ok with that way of living, then I'm ok with that. (Remember the title of this book… hint…hint).

But, if you aren't ok with that then it's time to change. Let me use myself as an example. Since the age of 14, I knew that I did not want to work a job. That feeling alone has lead me to quitting or being fired from over ten jobs. No matter how much I start off doing well at the job, eventually I become disinterested. My disinterest causes me to rebel from anyone trying to dictate my worth and how much should make. I know everyone is different, but working a job just does not fit me. Let me also say this- a job is a blessing and you should be grateful for where you are. I also know many people who love their jobs! The point is that if your heart desires more than that type of life-style, it's time to follow your heart.

Consider that God might be using your current lifestyle as a way to make you uncomfortable so you will want to enter in another season where your gifts can shine, where you find someone who loves you for who you truly are, or get the body you keep fantasizing about. Ultimately, there's nothing wrong with listening to that side of you that wants more. That's your higher self speaking to the current you!

Take The Time To Ask Yourself These Four Questions:

1. Am I satisfied with where I am at in my life right now?

2. Am I living or working towards my purpose or passion?

3. Do I wake up feeling free or feeling imprisoned?

4. Am I really happy at my career, social life, or in general?

If Any Of Your Answers Were Unsatisfactory, Then It's Time To:

1. **Self-Evaluate**

Assess here you are now. You cannot truly answer the question of why you are here if you don't know where to look. Start by evaluating and identifying areas that are holding you back by determining what needs to change in your life.

Here's another quick exercise. Jot down what you do not want in your life- whether it is spiritually, mentally, socially, physically, financially, etc.

Pause and look over what you've listed above. Now internalize how you feel looking over that list above. Take a mental screenshot of this list and repeat this to yourself: "I am now aware of the things I do not want in my life and I will work from this point forward to make sure I do not allow these things on my list to enter my life!"

2. **Get A Journal**

My mentor once said your journal is the textbook of your life-this is so true! Invest in journals and write down all of the things you like and dislike about yourself and in life as a whole. Try not to be too harsh with yourself in your journal, but be honest with yourself. Write as much as you can inside of it. Write down any business plans, strategies, thoughts, and experiences in your journal. This will serve as a reflection of your progression in life and will reveal if you are on track with your life goals.

3. **Create A Why Statement**

Your "Why Statement" should be a declaration to yourself. This will help remind you of why you are here and should be associated with your purpose. If your why for being successful is your children, to have a better home, to tithe more at church, to start a nonprofit, or whatever it may be, this will keep you accountable for the commitment you've made to yourself. Put your "Why Statement" in a common area where you will visit most. Your mirror, wallet, your screen saver on your laptop or cellphone are all good places to have it in. Your "Why Statement" should be clear, brief and true to you.

I've provided an example below to help you get this concept:

WHY STATEMENT EXAMPLE

"On this very day I choose to commit to my why. My why for going back to school is to further my education so that I can add more content to my Life Coaching business. I am dedicated to helping others succeed and I will make sure that when times get hard to remember that the reward of obtaining my Masters in Business Administration will be greater than any challenges I face. I am made for this and I have more than enough resources to get it done. I will go the extra mile and take the necessary steps to make sure that I graduate fall semester."

It's Your Turn!
Write Down Your Personal Why Statement Below

Take a moment to reflect on your statement above. Internalize what you've written down and make sure you put this in a place where you are reminded of your why. This will serve as your commitment that you made to yourself... besides who is better to bet on than yourself?

With the three suggestions listed above, you will be surely on your way to help assess you purpose, on addition to understanding key points to ensure that you are on the right path.

Let's wrap up Chapter one!

Let's summarize some key points from this chapter. To ensure you know the why for your purpose here on earth, first and foremost, get connected with your Higher Source, which may be God or whomever your spiritual teacher is. Use through prayer, meditation and stillness as a way to get connected and become clear in your life. If you don't believe in God, that's ok.

But please understand that there is a Higher Power than you and that you won't find that answer by yourself alone. Next, identify what you like to do and get a strong enough why for it. Once you know the why of what you are trying to pursue here on earth, the how will surely come. Furthermore, know the difference between Why Power vs. Will Power, and use them both to work together for your success! Finally, be sure to listen to your own dissatisfaction. I'm not saying focus on it entirely, however, if you are observant of all the things you don't like, you can watch out for them and choose to go another direction with your purpose. With all that in mind, I hope you are ready to walk into your purpose and calling!

"A MAN WHO HAS NO IMAGINATION HAS NO WINGS"

•••

Muhammad Ali

Chapter Two: Dreams Are Real

" Your ability to dream, puts us that much closer to the very nature of God"
~Lisa Nicole Cloud

If you want to transition into greatness, I dare you to dream. I believe dreamers can change the future and can advance all areas in human life. I was at a conference in Tampa, Florida last year where I heard Business Mogul, Lisa Nicole Cloud say, "Your ability to dream, puts you that much closer to the very nature of God." I know this to be very true. Dreams are spiritual and in order for them to become true we have to manifest them into existence. Now, I'm an amateur on the Bible, but I believe the Bible has some of the best life lessons and scenarios for the human experience. I also know that every time God wanted to communicate a message to someone in this book, he did it in a form of a dream or vision.

When He spoke to Abram in Genesis, He appeared to him in a vision or dream. In the same way, He does the same for all of us! Whether it's good or bad, I believe dreams come from the spiritual world. Here's how I know the power of a dream- you can visualize something even if you can't physically see it...and believe that something is there! I believe that alone is powerful! Dreams can also determine your reality.

I have to quote my pastor and friend, Rashiid K. Coleman, referencing a sermon he did this past New Year's Eve. He asked the congregation: "What do you see? What are you saying? And what are you doing?" I encourage you all to read Chapter 6 of Zechariah in the bible, to understand this concept. The underlying theme of dreaming comes from the pastor's first question, "What do you see?" Dreams are a form of seeing and seeing is very important to your transformation.

The real question is, what do you see in yourself ? When you look at your current situation what do YOU see? Are you looking at everything from your perspective or the lenses of a Higher Power? Do you see your life right now as your final destination? Or, are you looking at your life with the mind of an overcomer? Be careful that you are not limiting God's ability based on your limitations to dream. It's all about perspective and making minor adjustments to how you view your life. That's what dreamers are able to grasp- the concept of using the power of a dream and transforming it into a reality. It's now time for you to start doing the same.

There is also a negative side of dreaming. I don't want to talk too deeply on nightmares, but it would be naïve to say that they don't exist. Nightmares are considered to be unpleasant dreams essentially. It is smart, however to know that if you do have bad dreams, to use them as fuel to navigate into the positive. When I have nightmares, it's usually driven by a subconscious fear of mine.

Fear of defeat, poverty, disease and dying are what I consider to be nightmares. However, dreamers like myself, are aware of nightmares but are not shaken by them. Defeat, challenges, or adversity may come our way, but we know the value of what we possess and in due time we know it will come into existence. So don't be discouraged when you are faced with bad dreams- use them to transition from where you are now to who you are about to become! Allow your dreams to drive you and not to stop you. Besides, I will teach you how to overcome fear in chapter eight. For now, I have a few concepts to point out about the importance of dreaming that may be vital to your success.

DREAMS ARE SOMETHING MONEY CANNOT BUY

As I briefly stated before, I worked jobs that I hated. Not because the money was satisfactory, but because it wasn't in a field that I was passionate about. I found myself "job-hopping" or being fired from jobs because I would either stop caring or started to become insubordinate. I'm a true dreamer at heart and I know that I am, so no matter how much money I make, nothing can substitute the feeling of doing something I hate. I hated the feeling of being in the position where I did not want to be; it took me a while to figure why I felt this way about working for other people. Here is what I want you to know, if you are being forced to work somewhere because of monetary restraint, you will always be miserable.

Money isn't a bad thing, it is actually it's a great thing! I believe it's essential as the oxygen we take in, but money is not the key to permanent happiness. The key is to live a life you enjoy and to make your passion apart of your lifestyle, achieving your dreams and not the opposite way around. The outcome of your success will always be and feel better than the income. Chase your dreams first, and the money will come after.

"DREAM BIGGER, FASTER"

I heard a wealthy man say something similar to that phrase above back in 2014 on YouTube, when speaking to an audience about how he reached a pinnacle of success. He makes about 1 million dollars a month- yes a little over 1 million dol- lars a month and his key advice to the audience was that that if he were to begin his career again, he would have thought much bigger, much faster. Holton Buggs is his name- yes, Google him! The man lives like a king, and because of this, I know for a fact that he does not dream averagely or think the same way as an average person may think.

Similarly, I believe you too should start dreaming a lot bigger, a lot faster too. Why? Because it forces you to level up and step out of your comfort zone. Most people stop dreaming because they are simply comfortable and safe where they are. It takes faith and effort to stretch and go after your dreams. It can be discomforting at first- that's why people settle for average lives. When I say "average", I mean that you are not living the best life according to you.

Average does not necessarily mean external things like a fancy car or a big house. When I say average, I mean average in your thinking, average in playing safe, and being average in your actions. Being average is a choice, just like being extraordinary is a choice. We have been blessed with the power of choice, and I'm here to tell you, that nothing great has ever come from comfort zones or choosing to be average! If you want to transform into your own greatness it's going to require you to think and dream differently. The choice is yours.

DREAMS WILL BRING OUT THE BEST IN YOU

Back in November of 2015, I hosted my first event ever. It was a vision board party that I initially was going to do for myself. I've been creating vision boards since 2013, and I know the power in designing my future. That night, a thought appeared in my head to host a vision board party for the women within my Women's Empowerment organization called, "Queens See Queens LLC". I forgot I had written down a goal of hosting a vision board party, as being one of the things I wanted to accomplish in 2015. I wrote this goal down in my "*Step into Greatness Journa*l" by Entrepreneur and Community Activist, Nehemiah Davis. I turned my dream of having that vision board into reality. Was I scared? Yes! Did I doubt myself ? Absolutely. However, when I took myself out of the equation and channeled my focus on help-ing other women with their journeys, that fear of me fail-ing went away. Had I not hosted the vision board party and was selfish because of my own insecurities, I would have not been able to teach 30 women how to create their own vision boards that could potentially change their lives.

I would not have known my potential if I not at least attempted at it. Because of my dream, the women enjoyed themselves, connected with one another, cried, laughed and had a great time! If your dreams only benefit you, then they are too small. See our dreams will not only stretch us, it teaches us things we would have not known if we didn't take a shot to try. Allow you dreams to guide you into greatness.

CHARACTERISTICS OF A DREAMER

You may be wondering what skills one must have to be a dreamer. In order to be a dreamer you must be:

- **Optimistic**: Dreamers are hopeful and confident in themselves and the future.
- **Resilient**: Dreamers have thick skin and are able to bounce back from adversity.
- **Problem Solvers**: Dreamers always have ways to find an- swers to problems, by dreaming up a solution.
- **Determined**: Dreamers are driven by their dreams and
- are firm about obtaining them.
- **Consistent**: They are consistent with achieving their goals over a long periods of time.
- **Relentless**: Dreamers are persistent and are willing die for their dreams.
- **Committed**: They are dedicated to pursuing their dreams... no matter how long it takes.
- **Creative**: Dreamers are not limited to their creativity or artistic ways.

The world operates around dreamers. Either you are the dreamer or you work for one. So now the question is, are you considered a dreamer? Do you possess any of those characteristics above? Think about the greats, Martin Luther king, Beyoncé, Bill Gates, and Oprah Winfrey- they are just as human as you and I. The only difference is that they are living out there dreams or had a dream that has outlived them! Not only do the dreamers I just mentioned have those skills I listed above, but they also allow their dreams to bring out the best in themselves. So again, Why not you?

TIPS ON HOW TO DREAM BIG

Create a Raw list: write down an uncensored, detailed list of your dream life 5-10 years from now. This list should entail:

1. Where you want to live, the type of car you want to drive, where you would like to travel, etc.
2. The type of relationships you want to have.
3. The amount of income you want to generate and what type of industry you want to be in.
4. How you would feel and look.

*Be limitless to your dreams write it down with no restraints or guilt- remember this is your life!

____

____

____

How did that exercise make you feel? Do you feel empowered? Great! You must feel your dreams into existence. Act as if you are already in your dream life! I encourage you to keep this list and work towards actually making this list a reality. I would even challenge you to get a separate sheet of paper, type it out, frame your list, and hang it up as an inspiration toward your future. If you can believe that it can happen, it actually can happen. If you accept this to be true, you are one step closer to seeing your dreams manifest.

The universe just told me remind you with this question again: So, Why not you?

“THE ONLY THING WORSE THAN BEING BLIND IS HAVING SIGHT BUT NO VISION”

●●●

Helen Keller

Chapter Three: Visualize Success

"Everything starts with a vision"

If you want to truly transition into your own greatness, you must have a vision for yourself and for your future. Visions are very powerful and it's vital that you act on them as soon as they appear in your mind. What's so important about having a vision is that its serves as a navigation for your life. The visions that you may have are most of the time aligned with your purpose. As I mentioned in chapter one, finding your purpose has a lot to do with how you view yourself and your future.

Let me ask you this, when you come in the house from a long day of working, after putting in the key to open the door, what is the first thing you do? Turn on the lights perhaps? I would hope so! Now why would you turn on the lights? Is it so that you can see what's in front of you in order to move and get things done in the house? I would assume so! So, why is it that most people can turn on the lights to see inside of their home, but will not turn on the lights within themselves that could potentially unlock their purpose-filled future?

This is how most people operate. Most people go through life like the analogy above, except they operate in the dark. Why go around your house in the dark if you know you have the choice of turning on the light? It doesn't make sense, just as it doesn't make sense to not have a vision for your own life. Do not be the person operating in dark by not having a vision for yourself. If you are living and going through life in the dark, I ask that you create a vision. I don't care if it's to start your own book, towing business, or to just be a great parent, all of those things require vision. You must see the vision first in order to go after it and achieve it. Furthermore, where you are today is a direct reflection of your thoughts and visions from the past. If you want the next couple of years to look better than the last couple years, something in your vision needs to be adjusted. There is a saying that says that, "Insanity is doing the same thing over and over expecting different results". In order to change your future, modify the image of you future by visualizing success! How do you do that? First, let's break down exactly what vision really is.

What is vision? In this particular context, I believe that vision is seeing something before it happens, and having the option of making it a reality or not. We as humans have visions all the time- whether it's to start a new business, become a singer or actress, or become the greatest engineer of all time. Visions can either drive us into action or make us stagnant.

For most, visions can be frightening because some may think that they are incapable of achieving some of the visions that come to them. I remember seeing a quote posted on Instagram that read, "God will not put a vision inside of your heart that you cannot achieve." What a statement! When God drops and idea or vision inside of you, you have the choice at that moment to believe in the vision and to take action. It's all about what you believe about yourself that determines if you decide to go after the vision or not. Visions are just concepts created by the imagination and the spiritual realm. So the question to ask yourself is, what are you imagining? What are you dealing with spiritually? What are your thought patterns? Once you are aware of where your visions come from, you can change them to make a difference for yourself. Let me share with you a few reasons why visions are super important to your success story:

IMPORTANT REASONS FOR HAVING VISIONS OF SUCCESS

1. Visions serve as a navigation system for your life: Think of having a vision for yourself in the same way as using a GPS for directions to get to a place that you are unfamiliar with. Visions are the "Global Positioning System" for your life and you must have it in order to get to where your desired location is.

2.Visions can steer you away from returning to or going down the wrong path: Most people fail in life because they lack vision and opportunity. One way to ensure that you have a better life is to know how to make right decisions that will take you in the right direction towards your dreams. If you have a clear vision of success for yourself, you will recognize and steer away from paths and decisions that will subtract from what you intend on becoming.

3.With vision, you have a better chance at predicting the outcome of your success: Think about the "reaping and sowing" concept. You will see the long-term effects of your actions by the visions you choose to have today.

CREATE A VISION BOARD

This chapter of this book is called "Visualize Success" on purpose. If you want success you must see it for yourself first-I cannot stress this point enough. I believe vision boards are the perfect creative tools to make dreams a reality. What is a vision board? A vision board is used to help clarify, maintain and focus on specific life goals.
Vision boards can be used for multiple uses: accountability, inspiration, and positive affirmations. As mentioned before in chapter two, I started creating vision boards after I saw one on my friend's wall inside her room back in 2013. To me, I thought it was a poster board filled with fancy photos of materialistic things. Being the curious girl that I am, I asked my friend at the time why she had the board on her wall. She explained to me that her vision board was the "poster board" for her life in the next 3-5 years. I thought it was a unique and powerful concept to start implementing in my own life. From that day, I have created just about seven vision boards since 2013. I use vision boards to create my own success and to set immense goals. All vision boards can be utilized in many ways and depends on what your personal goals are. Vision boards can be used for all types of topics: business, personal, spiritual, mental, financial, or any area in life you wish to work on. The goal is to make vision boards accustomed to your own needs and wants. Vision boards can also be used for short term or long-term goals.

Vision boards can be measured monthly or yearly- it is completely up to you. If you see value in creating a board for your life, I encourage you to make one, and if you already are familiar with making vision boards, I encourage you to keep making them. Life is unpredictable and is constantly changing, so you want to make sure that you have some type of tool to keep you focused on your goals and aspirations. I believe vision boards are a great way to start.

VISION BOARDS CAN HELP:

1.**Provide Clarity-** This will help you become clear on what it is that you want from life.

2. **Increase Your Belief-** In this case, you will have to believe in the vision in order to receive what you desire and want from life.

3. **Drive You to Action-** Once you become inspired by all the things you put onto your vision board, it will drive you into taking action.

4. **Hold You Accountable -** This is of huge importance. There will come a point where you will become unmotivated, discouraged, and talk your way into thinking that your goals are too big or difficult to accomplish. Your vision board is there to remind you of the commitment you made to yourself and also the feeling that motivated you to making the vision board in the first place! Ac- countability will be the glue that keeps you attached to achieving your goals one step at a time.

Now that we understand the importance of a vision board, let's talk about the physical appearance of them.

In order to make a vision board you will need:

1. **Magazines**- Magazines are used to take out any images and words to help illustrate the life you want to depict on your board

2. **Poster Boards**- They serve as the background to your vision board. This is the platform in which you would post your images, affirmation words, and phrases on. I would suggest using bright colors or your favorite color (psychologically, colors brings out different feelings and you want your board to make you feel good).

3. **Scissors**- To help cut out all the pictures and phrases need to bring your board to life.

4. **Markers**- To outline, highlight, or add any additional affirmations and drawings to your vision board.

5. **Glue or Tape**- This will help conceal and secure any images from the magazines you place unto the board.

6. **Your Imagination**- Imagination is the secret sauce to making your vision board a complete success! Use it without limits!

Now that you know the materials to create a vision board, here are some tips dos for creating one.

YOUR VISION BOARDS SHOULD BE:

• **Neat and Clear**- Vision Boards are form of communicating to the universe what it is you want from life. If you have a neat and clear board that can be read, you are giving that same way of energy to the universe.

• **Selective and Meaningful**- I encourage you to not just put anything on your board. This is your life we are mapping out and should be taken seriously. Although this could be a fun thing to do, it is also important that you keep your goals in mind when choosing images and words to put on the vision board.

• **Filled with Images and Words that Best Represent Your Purpose and Ideal Future**- For instance, if owning a home in the next year is your goal, then having picture of the home you want should go on the board. I would even challenge you to go above and beyond by researching the home of your choice, find out the investment for the home, and create an action plan. If you do this, the universe will see that you are serious about your goals and success.

• **Inspiring and True to You**- This is very important. Before doing this activity, ask yourself what does success really mean to you? Don't feel ashamed or embarrassed of your goals because that's what you want for you. Don't compare goals and success to how other people may thin success is for you. Define your own success and bring that mentality to your vision board.

YOUR VISION BOARD SHOULD NOT BE:

• **Cluttered**- Cluttered equals confusion and that's not what you want to send to the universe. I know that may sound crazy, but think about a portrait you've seen that looked like too much was happening. Likewise, clutter on your vision board will cause you to think in that matter as well and will overwhelm you. Make sure your vision board is clear and easy to understand.

• **Negative**- If you place negative images on your board, that's what you will attract to you. Avoid negative pictures and letters when creating your masterpiece.

• **Rushed**- Take your time when your creating your boards, you want make sure you are putting thought and love into it. Don't rush the process.

• **Meaningless**- It wouldn't be wise to put up a board that didn't mean anything to you or to your future. Add meaning to your board-this is your life we're talking about!

HOMEWORK ASSIGNMENT

Now that you understand what vision boards are and how they can be important to your success story, I want you to create one for yourself ! Take time within the next week or so to create a vision board that illustrates the life you want within the next 12 months. I would first encourage you to write down your goals for the next 12 months on a separate sheet of paper and then transfer those goals on to your board. Be creative, fun and allow your creative potential to guide you during this activity. I would love to see your completed boards! Send pictures of your completed board to my personal email address: watersaja@gmail.com. I can't wait to see your masterpiece!

LIVE IN THE FUTURE

Visualizing success requires that we live in the future. I challenge you to use your imagination to create the life you want for yourself, even if your current reality says the opposite. I dare you to live in your future. I am a firm believer in this philosophy because I use my vision for my life to yield me to my future self. Some may call this, “Faking it until you make it.” I call it, “Show the universe that you are serious about the life you want by manifesting it until it comes into existence.” You have to walk, talk and act like a success, if that’s what you truly want. You don’t have to wait to start acting like what you want to attract. I’m not saying live above your means and go buy a purse tomorrow when you have other areas in your life that need attention. What I am saying is to start working on you so that the future you can handle the type of lifestyle you envision for yourself. There’s a quote that says: “Your future is hidden in your daily agenda.” It truly is. I wake up with my future on my mind. I look at my agenda for the day, as it’s aligned with the things I have planned for the future. My mentor Jim Rohn says that he can look at man’s ability to set goals and just off of that information can get an estimate of his bank account. That statement is a wakeup call to start now.

Start with what you have and use the resources made available to drive you into the person you want to become. It doesn’t matter if you have a hard life, we all have stories of that involves broken families, hurt, death, sickness, poverty, or guilt. Let those instances be even more of a motivator to work on your future now so that those things don’t become your end all be all. With all that in mind, I encourage you to have tunnel vision and stay the course of becoming the person you would see yourself being. To be honest, you are already who you envision yourself to be, it’s just inside of you, waiting to become free! I want you to repeat this statement: “If it’s to be, it is up to me.” This is the mantra I live by. If you want things to change, it’s time to stop second guessing yourself and step into your greatness. If you want to get out of debt, it's up to you. If you want to stop living in mediocrity, it's up to you. If you want to be a better person, it's up to you. Do you believe that? The biggest project you will ever work on is yourself, so if you are ready let's start working on your vision right now by believing what you see.

AJA'S ACRONYM OF VISION:

• **Visualization**: Visualize the life you want, and make the commitment to work hard until it becomes a reality.

• **Internalization**- Internalize that you will be successful. If can internalize success, it will show externally.

• **Summarization**- Summarize your life into one life mantra, and live by it. Here's mine: "If it's to be, it's up to me".

• **Implementation**- Don't waste your vision by not taking action. Implementation beats conversation. Don't just talk about your goals, implement them!

• **Organization**- Organize your vision by using tools and resources that will help you execute them in a timely fashion.

• **Navigation**- Navigate through life by allowing your vision to be "head lights" to your future.

In summary, we all have goals, dreams and aspirations we would like to achieve, but if we don't have the right tools or the vision to see it come through, you will have a much more difficult time making your dreams happen. We have directions for everything (how to fix a car, to bake a cake, to put up a table), but most people don't have the right directions for their own lives.

My goal is not to tell you how to live your life, but to encourage you to create your very own life using vision to take you there. Having a vision for yourself and the life you truly want has its ups and downs. People may criticize your vision and won't understand it either. Realize that the vision was given to you and you only, so everyone won't understand because it's not meant for them to understand it. Your goal is to go after your dreams anyway. It's vital that we all know the importance of having a strong vision for ourselves and stick to them, because visions can get lost or fade away. Vision boards can help prevent you from going off track with the commitments you made for yourself or getting back into old habits.

Again, the concept of having vision is simple but not easy. We're all dealing with life and the emotions, feelings, hardships and difficulties that come with it. The conditions we are born into are not our fault, but it is our fault if we choose to stay in them. That's why I wrote this book to begin with- to encourage you that you still can be and do all the things you wish to do if you have the vision to see it first. I believe in you, even if you don't believe in yourself. It took a while for my belief system to kick in and it's still an ongoing process. However, I believe in myself now more than ever because I trust God, I have confidence in myself and my vision, and I see where my future is taking me.

Transitioning from self-doubt into becoming the best you requires faith, confidence and belief. If you struggle with self-confidence, or believing in yourself, I say borrow the belief I have in you until your belief catches up.

One day you will be doing that for someone else! Remember, it's all about mindset, and I will go into more details in the next chapter. So again, Why not you?

"ONCE YOUR MINDSET CHANGES EVERYTHING ON THE OUTSIDE WILL CHANGE ALONG WITH IT"

•••

Steve Maraboli

Chapter Four: Mindset Makeover

" The same thinking that has lead you to where you are is not going to lead you to where you want to go." - Albert Einstein

Where you are today is a direct reflection of your thoughts years ago. I mentioned that statement earlier to reinforce that mindset is everything, especially if you want to transition from where you are to who you see yourself becoming. I want to start this chapter by breaking down the science of thinking the best way I know how. Your mind is the most powerful tool in your body. The brain, which contains all of our thoughts, is a very remarkable function. Thoughts are energy that is stored inside the brain, and energy is the power and force needed for continuous physical or mental activity. Energy is broken into the five senses, from which we learn everything from. Along with energy, the brain also stores thoughts that are broken into two categories: the conscious mind and the subconscious mind.

SUBCONSCIOUS VS. CONSCIOUS

The conscious mind is aware, awake and functions in "real time". I refer to the conscious mind as the "Lead singer", because that's the part of our brain that is upfront and in the "now". Your conscious mind reacts to your current decisions, actions and senses and is responsive to outside surroundings. The subconscious mind, on the other hand, is not so aware and is always influencing one's actions and feelings. I refer to the subconscious mind as the "Backup singer" because it's the thoughts hidden in the back of your brain working behind the scenes.

Your subconscious also works for your conscious, giving the subconscious instructions to obey and internalize. The subconscious mind additionally acts as a storage bank that keeps every experience and skill you have learned since birth. The types of thoughts or "instructions" that may go into the subconscious mind may be information you were told when you were younger, experiences from the environments you were raised in, and morals that you were taught by your parents or guardians.

Whatever information you put into your brain, the con- scious mind takes in, and tells the subconscious to put away for keeps. Why is all of that important? In order for you to change your way of thinking, it is vital to know where the source of your thinking comes from. Moreover, it would be wise to work on inputting the right decisions and actions you make moving forward, so that those actions will be directed to your conscious, stored into your subconscious, and result in positive outcomes. I want you to think of your mind as an empty glass. Take a second to ponder on all of the things, influences, voices, and experiences that have been poured inside of you from the day you were born until now. All of those influences have been programmed and entered into your "storage bank", the subconscious mind, and it effects how we interact and react to with yourself, and with the rest of the world. Knowing this, the goal now is to filter out and differentiate what type of influences are considered to be beneficial to your life and what needs to be replaced based on those type of influences and experiences. Now I can agree that as a child, it's pretty hard to control what's being poured into you because your parents or guardians were primarily responsible on how you learned and interacted. Just like traveling to a new country, as a child your mind is adjusting to the surroundings and environments around you. However, if you were raised in conditions where poverty, negativity, and bad energy were the norm, what type of affects do you think that may have had on your subconscious today as an adult? All of those years of negative influences, words, and energy are being poured into your subconscious- whether you know it or not. This may be why you have trouble communicating with others, you can only see the bad in people and situations, or you are afraid to take a leap of faith in your life.

That's why it takes a "village to raise a child". It's your thoughts that determine how you associate and interact with the world. This example may or may not apply to you specifically, but if you are a human being and live on planet earth, at one point in your life you have been at some point where you have been affected by some type of negative influence. We can't choose our parents, environment, or life…at first, and that's ok. It's no one's fault that the setup is the way it is, it's just called life and you cannot change the way you came into the world. My mentor Jim Rohm said, "Don't wish for things to be easier, wish that you were better." I would also add to that by saying to never wait on the world to change. Leave the ways of the world to the Creator.

I would suggest that you work on having the necessary tools to prepare you for what life has to bring- that starts with the way you think. If you understand that philosophy, and you are fully aware that how you used to think can't help you upgrade or progress through life, now you are well on your way. It's time to hit the reset button on the way that you think. Start to reprogram your mind by filtering out the old and replacing it with the new. The thoughts in your subconscious mind need to be replaced with things such as positive thinking, great books, prayer, and good thoughts. Understand that this transition is not going to happen overnight, but the goal is to cause a subconscious interruption in your thinking so that it reverses old habits into new habits.

I forgot to mention earlier in the context above that your subconscious mind does not know the difference between a positive or negative thought- it just takes in whatever it's been given. A thought, whether it's positive or negative in motion will continue unless stopped by an outside force. You are in control of how to handle that outside force and should monitor what goes in your brain and what goes out. Even to this very day I struggle with this, and I would be telling a lie if I acted as if I do not make mistakes when it comes to training my mind to think positively. In fact, I wouldn't be human if I just thought positive all of the time. No one is perfect, but the idea is to read this chapter as if you are already transitioning away from your old ways of thinking. It feels great to finally be awaken to what's possible and I hope by now you are on your way to unlocking what's been there the entire time. Remember it's the way you think that will determine the course of your future success.

PRACTICE POSITIVE THINKING

It's important to train your mind to see the good in every situation by practicing positive thinking. For example, let's say you find out that your best friend bails on you for dinner at the last minute. Now you can think and react to this in two ways: One way is to curse him or her out and rant about how this is the third time in your friendship that he or she bailed on you and blah, blah, blah. At that point, you are now in a negative state of mind and your whole day is ruined. Looking at this scenario from another viewpoint, you could simply say to yourself: "Hey although I am disappointed that my friend canceled our dinner, how can I see the good in this situation?"

Perhaps I can use this time to get some other things done or even take myself out to dinner!" See? It's all about perspective. I know it may seem cliché or "corny" in the beginning, but the goal at hand is to really train your mind to see the good in any situation. This is something I am working on myself, because at times I can be extremely petty and passive aggressive. However, when I feel my pettiness approaching, I stop myself and think before I act. Similarly, when you feel you are about to become negative or revert back into your old ways, interrupt that thought by replacing it with a positive thought. It is just that simple! Will it be hard? Absolutely! Is it attainable to change your ways of thinking? Of course! Understand that we live in a world where people will "try" you or you will come to a situation where you will be tested to see how much you've really changed. See it is in those moments of being tested where you have the opportunity to grow. When you do come to the point that something or someone tries to test you- be prepared and have your ammo ready. Never miss the opportunity on your chance to grow as a person. Practice putting good things in your mind until it becomes a habit. Just like you created the habits you have now, you can create new habits that can be beneficial for you. Got that? I know you can do it. The fact that you are investing in yourself by reading this book already puts you in the position to master the skill of positive thinking!

MINDSET MAKEOVER PROCEDURE

Now it's time for a mindset makeover! All of those gems I dropped on you will be of importance before going under this "mental surgery". Before I could give you treatment on how to start the process of changing how you think, I feel that it is important to know the science behind the way the brain works. The functions of your subconscious and conscious mind and how you convert negativity into positivity are vital to your mindset! I want to give you three suggestions to help cure your stinking thinking: whether it's your attitude, self-esteem, or whatever it is that is causing you to not be great-these suggestions may help!

CHANGE YOUR THOUGHT PATTERN

Ever hear the phrase, "As a man thinketh, so is he"? If you can control your thoughts, words and actions. Our reality is a mirror of our thought patterns. Let's first, ask yourself this, "Whose thought pattern am I embodying?" Is it the thoughts of your parents, teachers, or friends that you're a bi-product of ? Did you inherit your sassiness from your mother or your isolated manner from your father?

For instance, have you ever seen an overweight couple walking through the store and noticed that their child is overweight as well? An unhealthy morale or thought pattern has been passed down from the parents to that child. Don't take offense to what I am saying, but read my point from a logical stand point- the way we are now has been taught to us in some way, shape or form. Most reasons why we doubt ourselves because we are operating under someone else's thought patterns, and not our own. We've been taught how to doubt ourselves. I remember a time when I used to let people project on me the way they thought I should live my life, because I thought they knew more about me than I did myself. I lived like this the majority of my life trying to figure out why I was so unhappy and pretending to be someone I was not. I was a "people pleaser" until one day I said enough. Recently, I made the decision to eliminate the voices internally and externally that were not helpful to my success. I altered my thought patterns to listen to my true inner self, where God is, because that's where the answers really were all along. Once you make the decision to alter your thought patterns you will feel the weight of self-doubt come lifting off of you-I promise, but its starts with our thought patterns.

After you identify where your thought patterns are coming from, the next step is to adopt a new thought pattern. If you want to be successful, study those who are successful. If you want to think positive, practice positive thinking. If you want to be wealthy, study wealth. It's all mindset! Alter the way that you think by surrounding yourself with those who think positively; and be selective and careful of those you partake relationships in. It's easy to buy into other people's opinions and thought patterns, but if you want to change, you have to make alterations to your surroundings. Lastly, I suggest getting in the habit of inputting the right type of influences around you.

Reading books are also an effective way to help change your thought pattern. Choose books that caters to positive thinking. Listen to upbeat and impactful music. Engage in an audio books that teaches something or personal development. I'm not suggesting that you go cold turkey and cut out all the things you enjoy doing. I am encouraging take small steps that will drastically help the course of your purpose-filled journey. There's a difference between what we are trained to think and what the truth is. The truth is that your thought patterns must change in order for your life to change.

WORDS ARE POWERFUL TOOLS

Your words are powerful tools. Use them to create your future because what you say is what you get. This will also require practicing as well, but if you think good thoughts you are already in the right position to say the right words. Even today I have to use positive words to set the tone for the day. Declare that your day will be positive, productive and prosperous. Speak from a position of gratitude. You will only receive more if you are thankful for what you have. In- stead of saying "I have to go to work." Say, "I get to go to work." Change, "I have to pay my cell phone bill." to, "I get to pay my cell phone bill."

Minor adjustments to what we say can make a huge difference. It's all about the type of language we use. My mentor Jim Rohm says, "Don't be lazy in language". Use your words to attract the life what you want.

USE LAW OF ATTRACTION IN YOUR FAVOR

If you add emotion and feelings of gratitude and accomplishment in advance to your dreams, the universal law can attract that vision to reality. Wonder why not you? It's because your words aren't matching your thoughts. Belief has to be attached to what you say. You can't live the life you want and secretly don't believe that you can. The Law of Attraction doesn't work that way. What you focus on you create more of. If you focus on the negative, you will attract negative. If you focus on the positive, guess what?

That's what you will attract. This is a true quick story of how I used Law of Attraction in my favor. I was working at a hotel 3 years ago, and I had just got into Network Marketing as a part time source of income. My mentor at the time recommended a book called "The Secret" by Rhonda Byes which, talked about using Law of Attraction to obtain the "secret" to life's treasures. One day I needed 10 dollars to go to a business opportunity meeting as a representative of the company, but I didn't have it. So on my way to work I was thinking about how I was going to get that 10 extra dollars. I felt like I was going to get it even though I didn't know how it would happen. I know some of you are reading this thinking, why didn't I just ask someone for it, but at that time, I wanted to use Law of Attraction first. Not even a street block away from my job what was sitting on the ground? A crisp ten-dollar bill!

I was the only person outside, but to me that was my belief check that Law of Attraction is real. Point is, if I can use that power to attract 10 dollars to me, I surely can use that same law and apply it in all areas in my life- and you can too.

The importance of changing the way you think will ultimately determine how you operate throughout life. Thoughts eventually become true, whether it be directly or indirectly. You must learn to listen to your thoughts and eliminate all of the unnecessary junk in your head. Accepting and adapting to change is going to be difficult at first, but the reward of becoming a better person is what you should want for yourself. Below are some daily routines you can practice that can help reposition the way you think. As I mentioned before, your habits comes from your words, your words comes from your beliefs, and your beliefs come from how you think. So let's go over these suggestions:

AFFIRMATIONS

Affirmations are phrases that declare how you want your day to go. Affirmations creates and sets the tone for how you choose to look at the day. These statements can positively affect your perspective and change the course of any situation. In order for affirmations to work, you must believe and feel what you say. So if you are declaring that you are going to have a great day, but secretly feel like you are not, then the affirmation you stated will be ineffective. Below I want you to practice positive affirmations by creating your own. Use them to start your day and remember to add feeling to what you are saying.

Example: "I am beautiful/handsome and God has made unique and special. Today will be productive and positive and I can feel these words as I am saying them to become true."

3 Affirmations I Will Commit to and Say Every Day

____

____

____

You can choose and personalize your own sayings but make sure you believe what you say. That's the only way affirmations will work!

LISTEN TO SOMETHING POSITIVE 30 MINUTES A DAY

The internet is a lovely place, if you use it wisely. There are TONS of great materials on positive thinking and personal development. Use your headphones as a time to learn. Turn off the music in your car and turn on an audio on something positive. I'm telling you this is powerful stuff right here! Take any 30 minutes to an hour of your time every day and listen to Eric Thomas, Jim Rohm, John C Maxwell, etc. and watch a drastic change in how you think. You will thank me later!

READ SELF DEVELOPMENT BOOKS

Leaders are readers. There are millions of dollars that are invested in personal development. I suggest picking up a book and start working on you. This transition to step into your own greatness requires you to study so I recommend you start reading books like the one you are reading now! Go to your local bookstore, start browsing, and get your read on.

ELIMINATE NEGATIVE WORDS OUT OF YOUR VOCABULARY

Words and phrases such as, “I can’t”, “I don’t have enough of ”, “This is getting on my nerves”, “You’re stressing me out”, and “You make me sick” are detrimental and damaging to yourself. Negative words are like daggers to your future. Be careful of what you say because that is what you will get. Learn to use words to attract abundance instead of lack, love as opposed to hate, health instead of disease. Think before you speak and react. Always use words that express love, because love is the most powerful tool of all.

"WHEN THERE IS NO ENEMY WITHIN THE ENEMIES OUTSIDE CANNOT HURT YOU"

●●●

African Proverb

Chapter Five: Internal Battle (Whose Side Are You On?)

"Be careful of the thief on the streets that's trying to steal your purse, but also be aware of the thief in your mind that's trying to steal your purpose". - Jim Rohn

Sometimes your biggest critic and enemy is yourself. There's a book called "*What To Say When You Talk To Yourself.*", by Shad Helmstetter that I encourage you to read. It talks about the type of negative thoughts we program inside our minds that stops us from being our highest selves. By nature, one of the functionalities of the brain is to protect you from harm and danger. When you start doubting yourself and become fearful, your brain is focusing on loss aversion (which means to prefer avoiding losses to acquiring gains), and goes into protect mode. All that simply means is that there is a part of brain that psychologically chooses to stay stagnant as opposed to taking risks. In that manner, your brain goes down memory lane of all the failures you've had in the past in effort to keep you safe. That part of your brain unintentionally does this, however the end result is that you become stuck and unmotivated on perusing your dreams. Loss aversion causes people to hold back and to settle in their ways and habits.

For example, in the beginning of my entrepreneurial journey I spent half, if not almost of my time thinking in that manner. Whenever I would go out and talk about business to someone who I thought was very affluent and successful, I would shut down and talk myself out of a potential business partner or customer. Like myself, most people operate in loss aversion. Whenever something is too "risky" or "challenging", people automatically become afraid and think of all of the things that could possibly go wrong – which is natural. Some would call that way of thinking "safe", "logical", or "realistic". In some cases you have to think that way.

However, I believe you should not use logic or reality as a way to paralyze or keep you stagnant. That's how the war within you happens. You are resisting or fighting the part of you that wants more from life by using the tactic I mentioned above. This will only harm you instead of help you. The stories you tell yourself is where the battle goes on. When I say stories, I'm referring to the fearful conversations you tell yourselves about the things or situations that haven't come into existence yet. Can you recall a time in your life where you were about to do something and you got so scared that you talked yourself out it? That's what I mean by you're at war with yourself. It may not necessarily be the fear of doing something that keeps you from going after it, it's what you project and say to yourself that makes you not go after it-there's a difference. On the outside you may see normal, but on the inside you are at war with yourself. Thoughts such as: "You're fat", "You're ugly", "No one will ever love you if they found out who you really are", and, "You think you really can become a millionaire? You barely have twenty dollars in your account!", are all examples that typically stop people from moving forward with their dreams. Why does this happen? It's because those thoughts have been programmed in your mind that come from influences that are around you- and by default accept those thoughts to be true. Think about a popular song that is out right now. The radio station plays the record so much that you find yourself singing the tune of the song even when it's not playing. Radio stations do that to get you to buy songs and other music paraphernalia. Your brain is the same way. If you were told all your life that you were ugly, then most likely you're going to go around playing the tune in your head that you are ugly. The goal now is to change that station because its up to you to filter the tunes you decide to play in your mind.

Your parents, peers, religious teachers and society in general, has had an affect on how you operate and effects the conditioning of your mind. Why do they influence you? I mean these people are the ones that you trust, love and confide in right? See the key to this "internal battle" is to not only show your brain whose boss but to kill all of the outside voices as well, even if those voices comes from loved ones and friends. I have some great news for you, there's a way to fix this battle and conquer the enemy within- but first you must agree and decide that you want to put an end to this fight. Understand that you can't fight this battle alone and calling on God to help you will surely be the first stepping-stone to win the war within. Additionally, you must filter out the negative programming by knowing the truth about yourself- ask God to reveal the truth to you and go off what He says instead of what the world says. You can only be influenced by negativity if you accept negativity. If you don't know the truth, you can easily be swayed by what's not the truth.

Michael Jordan won six NBA championships, earned a total of fourteen MVP titles, and is named one of the greatest Basketball Players of all time. However, in the beginning of his journey, Michael was rejected from his high school varsity basketball team. What if Jordan would have listened to the voices around him and accepted that he wasn't a good player? Do you think he would be the legend he is today? Jordan almost bought into what his varsity basketball team told him. However, Jordan didn't let the team sell him on temporary defeat, and that is the same type of mindset you must have to win the war within. You have to become certain on who you are and make a decision to go after you dreams no matter how difficult it may seem at first. If God says you are the head and not the tail, then why keep living life as the tail? If God says you are a King or Queen, then why live life as if you are a peasant? Who we are is a direct reflection of our thoughts. It's time to get our minds in full armor and fight for our internal freedom! I have a few ways to show you how.

PERSONAL PHILOSOPHY

If you don't stand for something, you will fall for anything. Your personal philosophy serves as a guide to determine the choices you make. Your philosophy are morals, values and beliefs about yourself. The question is, what do you truly believe about yourself, your life and your future? If you are doubting your greatness, it's because that's what your personal philosophy is. If you are constantly downing your-self or living in your past failures, it is because you are not clear on how to go about changing this attitude about yourself. Your perspective on you serves as your navigation to help filter when opportunities or enemies present themselves in your life. Your philosophy is going to determine discipline that sets the tone for yourself and your future. It's now time to change what you believe about you and your future- if you choose to!

Write down your morals. If you don't have any, ,I would suggest creating some. After you've written your morals down, use them as a blueprint to help get your through life's ups and downs. If you want to be successful, you have to have a personal philosophy geared toward success.

GAIN CONTROL OF YOUR BRAIN

Show your brain who is boss. Don't become a victim of your mind and stop suffering in silence. There's an African Proverb that reads "If there is no enemy within, the enemy outside can do you no harm." Once you've mastered how to conquer the enemy inside of you, you have mastered the biggest part of the journey. That's all the battle really is; choosing what to accept and what not to accept inside your- self. Choose the side of you that says that you can instead of side that says you can't. Understand that you are not your mistakes, failures, or your past. So many of us get so infused and stuck on where we are that we get lost, and we think that that "moment" of failure or frustration is the rest of our lives- and it isn't. Enough is enough. It's time to show the "enemy" who's boss and kindly show that energy to the door. You can become and achieve everything you put your mind to- trust me. So, how do we do that? Learning and connecting with your spiritual self is the key to this internal battle, because your spirit is powerful than your mind and can conquer the chaos and confusion in your brain.

Additionally, start changing your perspective on situations, circumstances and the choices you've made or are about to make. Be willing to let go of the hurt and surrender to the side that is rooting for you. The same energy we use to input negativity inside of us is the same energy we can use to input positivity inside of us. That's why you have to practice positive thinking, affirming, and doing things that's going to add substance to your purpose.

Let's Try an Exercise. Take A Moment To Write Down And Answer These Questions:

What do really think about you?

____

____

____

____

How often do you spend negatively critiquing yourself and others?

____

____

____

How often do you feed into to negativity?

How much time do you spend watching, reading and listening to things that promote negativity

How often do you spend time improving yourself

Now take a moment to reflect on your answers. How you feel about them? I had you do that quick exercise to give you the ammunition to conquering the battle, by becoming aware of your habits that feed the enemy within. Own you're ugly parts of you. If you know the things that are holding you back, fix them! This will be important to your journey

COMPARISON IS THE THIEF OF JOY

Every second you spend comparing yourself to others is a second you could be using to improve yourself. When you compare yourself to others, all you are doing is comparing your disadvantages to their advantages, which falsely diminishes your own gifts. What we all fail to realize is that everyone goes through battles within themselves. We all have a story and we all have been in this position of self-doubt. Do you wonder why most people have low self-esteem or are un- grateful? It's because they are measuring their abilities and success to someone else's standards. I'm telling you that you will never be happy if you operate like this. Be in competition with yourself. Work on becoming better than you were yesterday.

Comparing yourself to others is a simple waste of time because it's all an allusion. With social media, the news and living in a society that praises outer beauty, it can be difficult to practice self- love. That's why I am encouraging you to work on you so that you know the truth about you- not anyone else's truth about you. It's what inside of you that not only brings out the best in yourself, but causes others to do the same. Instead of competing with others, collaborate with them. Learn from those who live lives that are exceptional and in abundance. Use and allow someone else's success to become proof that it's attainable. If you know who you are and your purpose, you will become unbothered about what other people are doing. Know your lane and understand that God made everyone's journeys different. Be thankful for the life you have right now and focus on being the best you.

TAKE THIS TIME TO WRITE DOWN ALL THE THINGS YOU LOVE ABOUT YOU!

List all of your attributes and the things you love about you below. *(Ex: I love the color of my skin, have the ability to humor others, and that I now have a degree in Business Administration)*

Write Down 3 Things That You Absolutely Love About You:

1.

2.

3.

I want you remember this quote: "The grass is greener where you water it". Don't waste time comparing yourself to others because it takes away from all the wonderful things God has given to you. You honor God by accepting who you are so work and build from just that.

DON'T LET TEMPORARY PAIN DISTRACT YOU FROM COMMITTING TO YOUR PURPOSE.

Change is constant. Who you were does not determine who you are. You are not your mistakes, pain or defeat. All of those things are just experiences that help us learn about who we are and grow from them. One of the many reasons why we have internal battles within ourselves is because we keep referring back to who we once were; not realizing that any past failure we've had does not determine who we are. Our pain, struggles and failures are not who we are. It's how we handle those factors that really defines us.

If you can understand this, you are one step closer to defeating the enemy with in. Whenever you feel yourself going back down memory lane, give yourself a pep talk. Remind yourself of where you are going and not where you've been!

"THE GRASS IS GREENER WHERE YOU WATER IT"

•••

Neil Barringham

Chapter Six: Creating a New You

" Allow greatness to become a part of who you are." -Aja Waters

I remember attending an event where one of my mentors at the time came to Philadelphia to train leaders on how to build a successful business. He was a guru when it came to personal development and used this as his foundation for his success. In his training he talked about dominating in all areas in life, which was one of his mantras. Dominating in all areas in life was the one message that stuck with me from his training. I remember him saying clear as day, "You can't be a successful business person and you're a bad employee, spouse, or parent". That message right there was all I needed to hear because it was a wakeup call for me. I had realized that all my life that I operated in this manner. I was good in one area of my life, but I was horrible in other areas. I was one way in front of my business partners but another way in my personal life. I was seeking change only in one area, not realizing that I had to change in every area in my life. See in order to have a whole, balanced and happy life, you must allow greatness become a part of who you are- period. You cannot expect greatness to appear in your life if you do not learn or study greatness.

I had to remind myself that how I do anything is how I do everything, so I had to create a new me. Similarly, in order for you to transition from doubt into greatness, it must first start with you.

OWN YOUR UGLY

The first step to creating a new you is to own your ugly. What I mean by this is that you have to accept and recognize where your flaws and weaknesses are. Why? So you know how to strengthen those areas in your life. Maya Angelou so eloquently stated that you must, "Do the best you can until you know better. Then when you know better, you do better." One area in my life that I considered "ugly" was being a huge procrastinator. For example, throughout grade school I always did great academically, however I started to slack off when I entered high school. When my grandmother, took (as people would say), "her elbow off of my neck ", I started to procrastinate and my grades started to reflect that. As a result, I started to see procrastination show up in areas of my life down the road.

When I started my business I had to take ownership of my ugly, and I had to pay for all those years where I did just enough, instead of going the extra mile. I had to learn and develop a new way of doing business, by tackling tasks when they first appeared, instead of waiting until the last minute and stressing myself out. I understand and accepted that area in my life that was "ugly" and I work on it everyday. I don't know what you "ugly" may be, however you must learn how to iden- tify it and start working on turning your bad habits in to good ones. How do you do this? Take time to have an honest moment with yourself.

Ask yourself: What areas in my life do I need to seriously need improvement? Is it your attitude that needs adjusting? Are you constantly seeking out opportunities to be negative? Are you a jerk in every relationship because you secretly fear rejection and love? It may be uncomfortable at first but, the goal is help identify what areas in your life that needs to be adjusted, so that you can create a new you.

Name 3 areas in your life that you need improvement in:

1.

2.

3.

REINVENT YOURSELF

Now that we've addressed areas in your life that may need improvement, it's time to reinvent yourself. This is not just a physical transformation, but more so an internal transformation. We have to work you internally so that the outside reflects what's coming from within. You can't be a millionaire with a minimum wage mindset. If I have not said it a million times already, your mindset will be the key to this process. You are what you think, so hopefully you've got that concept in your mental notes. In my journey of reinventing myself, many factors had to be taken into consideration: who I surrounded myself with, what I was putting my energy into, and what I truly thought about myself. It was hard in the beginning and it's still a struggle because I should always be working towards becoming a better person. Reinventing yourself may not be easy at first, but here are a few suggestions that helped me.

Being Open-Minded To New Opportunities: I had to get out of my comfort zone by trying new things, networking with people who had the same mentality as me, and reading up on topics that had to do with self- improvement.

Spending Time With Myself: I think that's where the real work came into place. When I spent time self- evaluating, I realized that there were a bunch of areas in my life I was in denial about. I wanted to become more valuable, but first I had to learn new habits to make me just that. You will have to develop new habits if you would like to be the person you see yourself becoming.

Hopefully those suggestions above can help you with reinventing yourself, because they have helped me tremendously. Practice spending time with yourself and trying new things and I can promise you will see change happen within yourself.

ADAPT A NEW LOOK

If I wanted to become successful, I had to look it and feel it. Your appearance says more about you than what you actually say. I'm not saying that you have to dress fancy, but how you look will determine how people will address you. You have to dress how you would like to be addressed, so whatever look you are going for, make sure it's neat, clean and presentable. Eighty percent of communication is non-verbal, so how you look speaks volume. Make sure you're communicating the right message.

TRUST THE PROCESS

Be patient with the process and allow gratitude to guide you into greatness. In the beginning of my journey, I used to think that I was going to become millionaire overnight. Then I realized quickly what it really takes to become a millionaire. It's a huge process becoming a millionaire. Although I am no- where near the million-dollar mark, that's still a personal goal of mine. Becoming a millionaire takes time, and until I reach that pinnacle, I need to work on de-veloping a millionaire mindset. The person I was meant to be and the dreams that comes along with it has everything to do with Gods time line and not my own. Ultimately, you want to be ready and pre-pared to be the person you see yourself becoming. You do not want to receive your blessing prematurely and you will not receive the blessing if you're not ready for it. Be patient with the process of meeting the right person, starting successful business, or whatever dreams you may have. For now, be grateful for what you have and you will receive more. Focus on working with what you have while reinventing the new you.

IT'S TIME TO BECOME THE SHIFT

Once you have accepted that there are some areas in your life that needs improvement, shift will happen. When you have an honest self-talk about where you need improvements in your life, the next step is to get prepared for a shift. All shifting really means is having a slight change in direction or position. So, perhaps there are minor adjustments that need to occur to see progress in your journey, such as waking up an hour early or eliminating soda from your diet. Once you decide that you are absolutely ready to make changes in your life, not only will that mindset take you to new heights, but it will also require three things of you:

1. **Mindset-** Mindset is the biggest part in the transition of who you are now to who you would like to become. If your mind isn't in the right position to change, the shift will not take place.

2. **Sacrifice and Commitment-** Once the shift takes place, it's important to stay the course with this transition. Be careful that when the shift happens that you do not slowly fall back into old habits and ways. Eric Thomas once said that in order to be successful, you have to be, "Able to sacrifice who you are now for who you'll become." In order to experience a shift in your life whether it's developing a new diet, skill or relationship, it requires commitment and sacrifice.

3.**Discipline-** Discipline is one of the secrets to becoming successful. Discipline will help you with maintaining the shift when it comes. Discipline will be the muscle to ensure that your shift will be sustainable. Overall, the change will happen once you are ready for it. If you have it made it up in your mind to move forward in your life, then the shift will work in your favor for your success!

Creating a new you will definitely be a part of the process and it will answer the question, "So, why not you?" It's all a learning process and will require small steps taken daily to create massive results. I can say that I am definitely not the same person I was a few years ago and I am still learning.
I am very young, I and have so much to learn about life. I would have never imagined writing a book this early in my life. However, I took the initiative to at least try to do it, and here I am! That's what you have to do for your goals as well! If I can do it, you can too! It all starts with thinking that you can and believing it to become true!

"INNOVATION IS REWARDED, EXECUTION IS WORSHIPPED"

●●●

Danny Gilbert

Chapter Seven: Take Action…Like Now!

" The distance between your dreams and reality is called action" - Unknown

Taking action will be one of the most important, if not the biggest measurements of your success story. The "transition" from being the person you are today into the person you see yourself becoming will require you to take action. If you want to step into your own greatness, you have to go after it- period. No matter how big or small your goals are, they are not going to handle themselves. In this chapter, I want to talk about the reasons why you may not choose to go after your dreams and provide some tips that will get you to take action

4 REASONS WHY PEOPLE DO NOT ACT ON THEIR DREAMS:

1. **Procrastination-** At some point in time we've all procrastinated-whether it was on an idea, task or challenge. The reality is that procrastination robs us of our future. Procrastination is the thief of success, and I will be the first to admit that I procrastinate on almost everything, so I know

the effects of this slow killer. Most reasons why people procrastinate are because they are fearful, overwhelmed, or their perspective on the task seems difficult.

2. **Fear**- This is probably the number one reason why people do not act on their dreams. Fear is just as strong as being paralyzed. People become fearful for many reasons, whether it be fear of the unknown, fear of failing or fear of change.

3. **Accountability**- Sometimes people will not take action because they don't have anyone holding them accountable to their dreams. Accountability is the glue to help keep your goals together to ensure that you achieve them.

4. **Your "Why" Is Too Weak**- Going back to chapter one, your why means everything when taking action. Most people are so quick to give up on their dreams because the "why" for achieving their dreams doesn't motive them enough to keep going. If your purpose or desire to change isn't strong enough, you will find excuses to stay where you are instead of executing. Of course I could go down the list of the many reasons why people do not take action, however I want to focus on ways to get you out of that phase, because taking action is the only way to measure your success.

BE A DOER INSTEAD OF A "SAYER"

Actions speaks louder than words. If you look at the top successful people in any industry, they have all mastered the habit of taking action. So why can't that be you? You too can be on top of whatever profession you desire if you decide to. The only factor that will take you to the next level in your life is to act on it. I am in total agreement with the philosophy that taking action supersedes talent, brilliance, or acquiring information.

Can you think of anyone you know that is just too smart for their own good? These type of people over thinks everything, and rarely takes action. Back in my old business, my partners and I used to diagnose people like that by saying they suffered from "Analysis Paralysis", because these type of individuals use their intelligence as a crutch instead of a resource. If you want to be great at anything, it requires you to use both your intellect and to take action- one cannot do without the other. The success equation goes like this: well planned ideas, plus execution, equals success.

Think about it, what's the point of getting a degree in business if you're not going to open a business? What sense does it make to invest thousands of dollars to hire a life coach and you do absolutely do anything with the information? I know that its "mind boggling" to some, but so many people do just this. They sit on their ideas and wonder why success isn't coming to them. Don't be like those people. Instead, let your moves do the talking for you. Success is something you attract by attracting to it. Get in the habit of making more moves and saying less announcements, so that success will find its way to you.

SET GOALS AND WORK SYSTEMATICALLY

Have you ever heard the phrase, "A dream without a plan is just a wish?" Whoever said this was very wise, because this is so true. If you fail to plan, you simply plan to fail. Goals serve as check points to ensure that you are on the right track to achieving your dreams. If you don't have the right plan, how will you get there? Even God the Almighty has a plan, so why don't you have a plan for yourself ? It's not enough to just have a plan- work it systematically. Create a strategic action plan so that you can make the process a smooth one. Whether you decide to have a plan or not, there will be results for what you choose and choose not to do. Hopefully, you are reading this book because you would like to have a plan or even perhaps enhance your plan- because it is very important to have one.

DON'T THINK IT, INK IT!

Don't rely on your mind to remember your ideas. Record every aspect of the ideas that comes to you. It's so vital that you write down your goals the moment they appear in your mind, because just as an idea can appear, it can easily vanish. Earlier in the book, I mentioned the importance of keeping a journal to avoid this happening to you. Treat your goals as though they are a deposit to your success. Every time you get an idea, write it down. When you think of an idea say, "Another idea, another million", or however much you think your goals are worth. Furthermore, I want you to get in the habit of writing your goals down so that you can either refer back to them or get started on them right away. I remember back in February of 2015, I had been fired from my job and was denied from unemployment.

I was depressed, desperate, and hurt because I thought to myself "I let myself down again".

All I could at that moment was self-evaluate my errors, pray for understanding, and ask God to help me. I had to learn from my temporary failure and become better than the situation. After I had done all of that, I reached out to a friend and mentor of mine, Marsha, because she is successful and I admire her. She agreed to have lunch with me and I bought my journal with me to write down information from the meeting. After I told her about where I was in my life and inquired if she could possibly help with employment, she asked me what were my goals and passions. Next, she had me write down the top four things I like to do, and things that I am good at. Before meeting with her, I did not have those things written down, but I had an idea of those things. To make a long story short, she reminded me of the importance of writing down my goals. One of the things that I wrote on my list was that I wanted to become a speaker, because I like to inspire others.

Fast forward to today, I now have spoken in over five schools since last year and have been asked to be a panelist at a Women's Conference in May of this year. There's something magical that happens when you put ink on paper- and you believe what you write down. I encourage you, to write down your goals. I don't care what life throws at you, design your own future by goal setting as a way to create your future.

HAVE SMART GOALS

If you're a fan of self-help books like myself, then you have seen or heard of the acronym called, "SMART Goals". SMART Goals are one of the many systematical ways to help jump start you into action.

The Acronym "SMART" stands for Specific, Measurable, Achievable, Realistic and Time Bound. I will break down below how you can use this goal setting tool in your favor.

- **Specific**- The goals you write down should be exact and true to you.

- **Measurable**- It's important that any idea, goal or dream that you have is measured to some extent. Set deadlines, get organized and track your progress.

- **Achievable**- You never want to set goals too high or too low. Make sure you break down your goals in baby steps and gradually add on to what you've achieved.

- **Realistic**- Piggybacking off of ensuring that your goals are achievable, make sure that they are also realistic. If one of your goals for example is to own a Lamborghini by the end of the month, but you still don't have your driving permit, then you have to become real with where you are and understand that any goals requires a process.

- **Time Bound**- Time is one of the biggest assets we have while we are here. Take advantage by making sure that your goals low with the time that has been given to us by God.

DON'T STOP UNTIL

When it comes to your goals, train your mind to see your goals to the end. I read an article in Success Magazine a couple years ago about goal setting, and one of the subcategories of the article goal read, "Don't Stop Until…" I found that subtitle interesting and made it apart of one my life mantras. Don't stop until you get what you came for- whether its until you pay off your debt, become a millionaire, get your college degree, stop living paycheck to paycheck, or to lose 40lbs. Develop the mentality of "I will not stop chasing my goals no matter what it takes," because life will test you to see if you really are serious about what you want from life. How you respond to life is first asking, " So, why not me?" Then strive to achieve your goals until life works for you and not against you.

BE COMMITTED AND CONSISTENT

Commitment is doing the things you said you were going to do, even when the mood you said it in has left you. You have to dedicate everything to your dreams, if you are serious. This is not a book out there for those who sort of want to be great, but not so much- NO. I want you to read this book with an "I'm ready to step into my own greatness" type of mentality, because that's what's going to drive you into action. Commitment and consistency is key. No one takes an inconsistent person serious. It's time to start making moves that will ensure that you will be a success! Anytime I ask that question, "Why not me?" and the context is coming from the feeling of failing at something, I channel my secret shifter.

My secret shifter is another word for my "why" and keeps me committed to my goals. Want to know my secret shifter? When I'm feeling discouraged or feel like I'm ready to quit, first I think about God. I ask God to help me get out of the mentality of operating as a victim to a situation or circumstance. Next, I think about my haters. I think of all the things people say that I am incapable of achieving. This fuels me into action. I also think about who I am letting down if I don't follow my dreams. I don't have children, but I think about my unborn child all the time. I know the things that I do now will affect them when they do arrive. For you, you have to dig deep and channel your secret shifters. What is your secret shifter? Is it your children? Your income? Your spouse? Your haters? I don't care what it is but find something that will give you that spark of committing to your future success.

Being consistent is another part of measuring your success. To be honest, success is really a form of measurement. What you simply put in, will be your outcome. When I think of consistency, I think of the owner of Kentucky Fried Chicken, Mr. Colonel Harland Sanders. He started his first restaurant business in 1935 and closed it in 1952. Although he "failed" with his first business, he kept going. His actual success didn't come until 1964, when he acquired more than 600 franchised restaurant outlets, selling his interest in the company for $2 million to "Kentucky Fried Chicken" went public in 1966 with more than 3,500 franchised and company-owned restaurants worldwide, at 74 years old.

This a perfect example of consistency being used in Sanders favor. Mr. Sanders was determined, committed and consistent with his business starting off by making batches of chicken and selling his chicken to restaurants for only a nickel and becoming a multi-millionaire at age 74. In conclusion, success doesn't care how old you are, where you come from, or color of the skin- what it cares about is how hungry you are about obtaining it. One of Sanders famous quotes are: "There's no reason to be the richest man in the cemetery. You can't do any business from there." If you feel like success isn't in your alley, think about Colonel Sanders story, and borrow his belief- if he can be great at the age of 74, so can you.

PRODUCTIVITY VS. ACTIVITY

The subtopic above is gem galore- the title itself is self-explanatory. I remember listening to an audio from bestselling author and entrepreneur Darren Hardy called "*Making the Shift: Developing the Entrepreneurial Mindset*". As he begins to talk about the obstacles that will be faced transitioning into becoming an entrepreneur, he refers to obstacles one may face as "land mines". One of the "land mines" he warns the listeners about in the audio is to never mistake activity with productivity and movement with achievement. When I heard that philosophy back in 2013, it blew me away. All my life I used to do things that had nothing to do with my goals. Back in high school, if I had to do my homework, I would start on it, then drift off...finding myself organizing folders, instead of actually doing my homework. I would distract myself from actually working by doing unnecessary "busy work".

I ask that you don't make the same mistakes I made because those habits will sooner or later catch up to you. Make sure that the actions steps you are taking are geared towards your greatness. Additionally, never confuse movement with achievement. It's nice to celebrate small wins, but then it's back to work! I encourage you to utilize every moment to help you become a better you. Short term sacrifices for long term success starts with executing your goals now! Here is a tip to help you take quality action steps. Every night before you go to sleep write down your to do list in your planner or journal. Your to-do list will be the last thing on your mind and the first thing when you wake up- which means you will have a head start on the next day! Try it and see if this may help! Remember, how you do anything is how you do everything and creating a to- do list will keep you on track on being productive and not "busy".

Overall, taking action will require you to just take action. Don't think too hard on it or contemplate about it-just do it. If you want to be successful, just do it. If you want to write a book- just do it. If you want to lose weight- just do it! Just start. You don't have to be perfect to start, just start. There will never be the right time to get started, and if you think that there will be, you are wasting your time. Take action... like now! Put in the necessary work now so at the end you can celebrate instead of explaining.

Let me also tell you, when you finally face your fear, it's one of the greatest feelings in the world and I am glad that I decided to face my fear of heights! Although that's one small example of the many fears I had to face, I wanted to show you and encourage you to take the risk of overcoming your own fears so that you too can finally break free. Let's talk about you now. What exactly are you afraid of ? Is it Public Speaking? Going after your dreams? Quitting your job to become a full time entrepreneur? To fall in love? Let me ask, so, why not you? What's stopping you?

I am asking you rhetorical questions to have you think deeply about what's holding you back from being and having all that you truly want. I want you to understand that fear is a mechanism that is used to control you and keep you in mediocrity. I wouldn't want anything "average" for you or anyone else. I truly believe that we all have greatness within us all; everything you want is on the other side of fear.

What's causing you to operate in fear and to doubt yourself has a lot to do with the stories you are telling yourself. All of us, at one point in our lives have made excuses or stories for why it's ok to operate in fear. I remember in my early stages of becoming an entrepreneur, I was looking to develop a team of leaders to do business with. I had an opportunity to make substantial income with an accredited business and I wanted to expand. When I would talk to people about the opportunity however, they would turn it down. I used to get so upset about this, because I hated dealing with rejection. I had to learn that it wasn't the opportunity that the people I went to were turning down - they were turning down themselves. I had to understand that the people who believed

"THE BIGGEST MISTAKE YOU CAN MAKE IN LIFE IS TO BE CONTINUALLY FEARING YOU WILL MAKE ONE"

•••

Elbert Hubbard

Chapter Eight: The F Word(s)

" Sometimes what you fear the most is the very thing that will set you free." -Robert Tam

Have you ever been in a terrifying situation to try something new or different? When everything was over, did you sud- denly realize that what you were going though wasn't so bad after all? That feeling you've experienced in that situation is called fear. Fear simply means, "False evidence appearing to be real". Most people are fearful of failure and change. I'll be the first to tell you that Fear is FAKE. It is an allusion from the imagination that makes reality appear scarier than what it is. For instance, one of my biggest fears used to be heights. I used to be afraid of roller coasters, airplanes, and walking up vast flights of steps. My fear was that I might, in any of those situations, slip by accident, fall, break my neck, crash, or die. The reality is that all of those things could potentially happen in any of those instances, but it is still considered to be false evidence until it actually happens. The aftermath is something my imagination made up to keep me from "hurting myself " but it is not real. After understanding that, I overcame my fear of heights because I was tired of holding out on things that potentially could be fun, adventurous and not so bad after all.

the opportunity was not for them, were for personal reasons, and had nothing to do with me. I needed to stop telling myself "stories" about something being wrong with me, because it wasn't. Fear is a choice, and the point I am trying to make is that you can't allow the stories you tell yourself to keep you from moving forward. If you are experiencing fear while you are about to pursue your dreams, do it any way. The world is ran by those who move in faith and belief and not the opposite. Why can't that be you? You too can choose to use faith instead of fear-the choice is yours. My goal in this chapter is to inform you on how to recognize your fears, and give you tips on how to prepare and conquer them when the feeling arises.

HOW TO OVERCOME FEAR:

Pray: Pray: Use prayer as a guiding tool to ask how to overcome specific fears. If you believe in God, ask God to give you courage and increase your faith so that you are able to face your fears. If you are not a spiritual person, I encourage you to meditate-in some ways meditating is similar to praying. Use prayer to channel the inner you so that you are able to seek answers to help overcome the fear and decide the route you decide to choose.

Breathe: Breathing is one of the most powerful, yet simple ways to conquer your fear. When you breathe in and out, by default it calms you down and allows your body to become in tune and aware. Breathing can set you free and helps focus on the present. It can defeat any fears that you are facing. Next time you are faced with anxiety or fear, just stop, pause and take a deep breath. Focus on the present. It can defeat any fears that you are facing. Next time you are faced with anxiety or fear, just stop, pause and take a deep breath.

Release Control: This is a big one-even for myself. For instance, I used to be a control freak and in most cases this was a bad thing. I used control to disguise my fears- especially in my relationships with others. My goal in doing this was to avoid becoming hurt by others. I would try to manipulate and dominate my significant others so that I could feel powerful. That was the wrong type of mindset I had and it resulted in toxic relationships. In reality, you honestly can't control or predict everything- it's impossible. That is something that I am still learning today. My best advice if this pertains to you, is to get rid of the illusion of being in control, because in this context, it is considered a form of fear. Set yourself free and just go with the flow of things. I am not saying to be careless, but give up the things you have no control over and work on the things you can.

Adjust Your Perspective: I talked about perspective in almost every chapter of this book because that's what it's all about. If you want to overcome fear, you have to adjust your lenses on what you see as fearful. It's all about mindset, and if you have a negative mind, surely fear will take its toll on you. Sometimes we focus on the negative and what could go wrong instead of looking at all options. If you are not careful, this will cause you to assume and jump to conclusions about things that are not at that moment evident. You cannot make a final decision without looking at all options in all aspects. Change your perspective before you choose fear as your final answer.

Take Action: Feel the fear and do it anyway! Just do it and get it done. Your desire to want to be and do more has to be greater than your fear. What if the slaves gave up in the middle passage? What if they decided to settle for being mistreated in the type of conditions that they were in? They did not give up and fought for over 400 years to become free- their faith was bigger than their fears. The slaves knew that one day soon they would become free. That's deep- and some people won't even attempt to try to become great in all that they do with the freedom that they have! I encourage you to take action immediately because fear will always be there, especially if you keep entertaining it. When you take action your fears become weaker because at that point you're letting fear know that you are stronger than it- and guess what? You are! Start now. I promise you the more actions you take the less you will feel fearful.

Understand Failure: Failure is only temporary and should viewed be as a learning experience and not permanent defeat. Failure is just a way to redirect your path or strategy. You will learn more from your losses than you do from your gains- trust me. I remember going to a conference in Miami, Florida where one of my mentors Robert Kiyosaki said, "The only reason why I am more successful than you is because I failed faster." That was my aha moment for me. It was at that moment I realized that failures will only teach and gear me into the right direction. If you are afraid to fail and decide not to move forward, you will always be in the same condition that you are in. Don't let the fear of failing paralyze you- failure is there to help you grow and learn from your mistakes.

FAITH ARE THE NEW WINGS

There's another "F" word that I would like to elaborate on, to help assist you with your transformation is called faith. Faith is a magical and powerful tool and is the bridge that will take your from where you are now, to where you see yourself in the future. Having faith means you have complete trust or confidence in someone or something. In my opinion, faith is your way of telling God, "I trust you and I am ready to be led by you." I can't even begin to tell how many times faith has gotten me out of debt, broken hearts, disappointments, and tight situations. Whenever I felt defeated, I used faith as my way of knowing that better days are coming and that God will help me with whatever I was facing. If you truly want to overcome fear when it appears, you must exercise your faith muscles. Whenever you feel like you're about to face adversity or fear I want you faith it until you make it. Faith is truly the new wings, and if you want to fly and be free you must use them.

HERE'S A QUICK EXERCISE:

I want you to list the top three things you are afraid of or that's preventing you from achieving your goals:

1. ______________________________

2. ______________________________

3. ______________________________

Next, I want you to write down the top five things you would be or have if knew you could not fail:

1. ______________________________

2. ______________________________

3 ______________________________

4. ______________________________

5. ______________________________

Finally, I want you to look at both lists and ask yourself which list you would rather be pursuing. Is it the first list or the second list? If you choose the second list, I want you to make no excuses to getting those things done. You only get one life. How would you feel if you were in your final days, you look back, and see that you let you and everyone else down; because you were too afraid to be all that you could be? No one ever remembers the person who gave up on their dreams by quitting or feeling sorry for themselves. You are a winner. You were born to win and winners do not think about losing. Choose to win by telling fear that it has to go! Now that you know the "F" words, I hope that you will choose the right word that is suitable for you.

"DON'T LET SOMEONE WHO GAVE UP ON THEIR DREAMS TALK YOU OUT OF YOURS"

●●●

Unknown

Chapter Nine: Haters? We All Have Them

"Be So Good That They Can't Ignore You"
- Steve Martin

This will probably be the shortest chapter in the book. I designed it that way so that I don't spend too much time elaborating on this. It's necessary to bring this up because you will come across haters. Haters are everywhere and will be a part of your journey to success- especially if you're on to something great. I want to give you some details about who they are, the roles that they play, and how you should handle them.

Haters are negative people that are always looking for people to join their parade. They hate to see you or any other person doing something great because it makes them look small or mirrors the insecurities within themselves. Haters can be upfront or indirect about their strong feelings towards you- either way your heart will alert you. Haters can be strangers, co- workers, friends or "frenemies", family members, spouses, and even yourself.

THERE ARE MANY WAYS YOU CAN IDENTIFY A HATER:

1. **Direct Hater-** Someone who talks badly to you or about you every chance they get.

2. **The Indirect Hater-** Someone who subliminally hates on you or likes to "throws shade" on you all day, every day.

3. **The Pretender-**This is someone who pretends to your friend or on your side, but are secretly praying for your down fall.

If you haven't experienced hatred from any of those types of people, sooner or later you will. Let me start off by saying that hater's intentions are to make themselves feel better by trying to degrade you or your dreams. For example, let's say you want to start a new business and you tell your "friend" about your exciting venture, and their response to you is, "A business? Why would you want to do that?" Or may say, "Oh, my aunt started a business before and she's still struggling." Understand in this in- stance that your "friend" is hating. In your mind, you would think that since that's your "friend" supposedly, and that he or she should be as happy about your new venture as you are! Let me tell you, don't take it personal or dwell on their thoughts for too long because it will drain you. To be honest, the opinions of others have nothing to do with you but everything to do with that person.

Never let a hater's limitations block you from achieving your goals- no matter who it is. Understand that hate is also an expression of fear and most of the world operates in that manner. For the most part, people don't know that they're "hating" and will try to use it to try to "protect" you by making sure you play it safe. On your way to success, if you ever come across someone telling you why you shouldn't be going after your dreams, most likely they speaking out of fear. Recognize it and keep it moving. If your dreams aren't to hurt or harm any- thing or anyone, why not go after them?! Be mindful to always take advice and not order, and of you are taking advice, make sure that it is not coming from a hater.

Next, let me give you insight about a story in the Bible called, "Cain and Abel". This story was one of the first stories on betrayal and hate and it's best way I could illustrate this topic. Cain and Abel were sons of Adam and Eve. Cain was a crop farmer and Abel was young Shepard. God was pleased with the works performed by Abel and not so pleased with the works of Cain. Cain became upset with God's judgment of their jobs and became jealous of Abel. Instead of Cain finding ways to improve his works, he killed his own brother Abel out of hate and jealousy. God sees all of this, and asked Cain where his brother was after he murdered him. Cain replied with one of the infamous lines: "I am not my brother's keeper." God was not pleased with what Cain had done to his brother and punished him by cursing him and future generations after him. The moral of the story is that God will surely handle your haters. When haters try to "kill" or "murder" your dreams, God will take care of them. Your job is to keep shining and working. On the flip side, do not become a hater yourself. If you ever catch yourself hating on someone, stop and ask yourself: What is it about this person that I am jealous of? Why am I hating on them? Ask God to take the hate out of your heart and get into gratitude mode because being a hater will block your blessings. Lastly, hating on who you are is an insult to God and the universe. When you practice self-hate towards yourself it's considered to be selfish and unappreciative- all of which will never allow you to step into your own greatness. You will never receive an abundance of all the things you truly want for your life if you are hating on yourself-whose side are you on? Hopefully by now in this book you are transitioning from a place of uncertainty to a place of confidence. The same energy you use to feel like you are unworthy can now be reversed into feeling like you are worth more and deserve more. Learn to love yourself, because that is the only person you have to truly live with. Choose you and never let anyone or anything stop you from achieving greatness.

HERE'S ARE A FEW TIPS ON HOW TO DEAL WITH DIFFERENT TYPES OF HATE

HOW TO DEAL WITH SELF-HATE

1. Forgive yourself. We are all human at the end of it all. Hating yourself does not solve anything.

2. Stop using language to break yourself down. Instead use words to build you up. If you are the person who's con- stantly joking and insulting yourself- stop it. It's not at- tractive and will not give you the confidence you need to your transformation. Replace those words with positive affirmations and declarations.

3. Disengage yourself from activities that do not serve you. This means disengaging from anything that distracts you from committing to your purpose. If it's watching TV, eating unhealthy foods, or partaking in negative relationships, you have to cut ties with these types of things or limit yourself to it. Remember you want to add value to yourself, and not subtract from it.

HOW TO DEAL WITH PEOPLE WHO ARE CLOSE TO YOU THAT ARE UNSUPPORTIVE OF YOUR DREAMS

Learn the Law of Disassociation. I learned this law from Holton Buggs, who I previously mentioned in Chapter 4. I was on YouTube, watching Buggs at Eric Worre's "*Network Marketing Pro Expo*" in Las Vegas of 2014, when I watched him talk about the Law of Disassociation. This law simply means to separate or disassociate from people who are not evolving with you or with where you are going. This includes parents, friends, spouse or whomever. Now, that doesn't mean that you cannot love and care for these people, but you have to do it from a distance.

Law of Disassociation is only used so that your energy is focused on your dreams and not to get distracted. If they are not going where you're going, it's time to leave the nest and try your wings. On your way to success you will lose friends and family members and that's ok. Love them from a distance and do not take it personal. Work so hard on your dreams that you turn your family and friends from skeptics into believers, and I promise you they will be come back into your life on a different note.

HOW TO DEAL WITH OUTSIDE HATERS

Don't. That's not your job. Your job is to focus on your goals and let God handle the rest. No need respond or react to every person who has something negative to say about you or what you are evolving into. Besides, if you try to get at every bird (hater) that is trying to take away your crops (dreams), you leave your field (purpose). Pray for them and keep focusing on your goals.

"LIFE IS 10% WHAT HAPPENS TO ME AND 90% OF HOW I REACT TO IT"

●●●

Charles Swindoll

Chapter Ten: Situation-ships

"It's not the condition of the boat, but the set of the sail" - Jim Rohn

I quoted a phrase in chapter one that said, "Life isn't wrapped in the prettiest box, but it's still considered a gift." In my honest opinion, we couldn't be living in a better time than right now. We have all of the guidance, resources, and tools needed to help prepare us for the great things, and not so great things that comes with life. I'm assuming by reading this book, you are at a point in your life where you are ready to take initiative, take action and start working towards your goals. You have it in your mind to win and you are ready. Now, what happens when you are working towards your dreams, and the bad side of life kicks in? What do you do when failure and defeat are looking you right in the face? You're doing every- thing right, you're applying all the things I have suggested, and you've been working on yourself and goals-then suddenly life happens to you. What do you do? All of a sudden someone dies that was near and dear to your heart. You start getting those student loans after six months of graduating and still not finding a job in your profession. You get pregnant too soon, and the person who you loved so much wakes up and leaves you.

You go from, “So why not me?” to“ Why me?!” In this chapter, I want to be as transparent as possible because it will be in those moments above where your faith, goals, and growth will be tested. I cannot tell you specifically what to do in every situation, however I can suggest ways to help prepare you for when life happens- because it’s going to happen on your way to success. Don’t let this discourage you. Get in the mindset of becoming ready for whatever life throws at you because this will help you grow into your success story.

“ADVERSITY WILL INTRODUCE A MAN TO HIMSELF”

I remember seeing the quote above by Albert Einstein not too long ago on Facebook, and all I could say was “ Yessssss”, because I would not be who I am today if it weren’t for the challenges, adversities and failures in my life that I had to overcome. In my 22 years of existence, I had to quickly learn the importance of being resilient from setbacks in my life. One of those setbacks came from being homeless. At the age of 19, my grandfather, who I was living with at the time, kicked me out and put my belongings in the street because someone took $165 out of his dresser and accused me of it. Before that moment, everything was going well. I was working, started a new business venture, and I was happy and comfortable. Life came and hit me like never before. I was more hurt than anything because I knew I did not take money from him. My livelihood was measured by $165, and I had no savings or emergency funds to help me out. I had to think quickly on my feet because I had nowhere to go. I called my friend and her mother came and got me from my grandfather’s. I stayed with her for about three weeks.

The other two weeks, I stayed in a shelter for homeless young adults. I felt defeated and lost. I didn't understand why God would throw a wrench in my life such as that, and I nearly sunk into depression. At that moment, I felt like I had lost it all. Something happened to me in those two weeks of being out on the streets. It humbled me like never before. It almost felt like I was in prison at first- having someone tell you what time you had to go to bed, when to eat and taking 75% of your paycheck so that you can save for an apartment. I was hurt. I did not realize how ungrateful and carless I was until I became homeless. Seeing the young adults at the shelter with literally nothing was a serious wake up call. I knew that if I did not change my ways that this could be an outcome for me.

After thinking that, suddenly my perspective changed. Instead of spending my time pondering on what happened, I used those two weeks as an opportunity to discipline myself and get out of that situation. I used that time to get closer to God. I had told absolutely no one that I was living in a shelter with the exception of my friend and mentor at the time. I was too ashamed to tell my story. What I did not know was that my story could benefit and help someone who may have gone through a hard time such as this. After that experience, I was able to get my first apartment, get back on my feet and I never turned back- through the grace of God of course. I told myself that I would never allow myself to get that low again. Looking back from that situation, I now believe it was one of the best experiences ever because it exposed me to who I was at the time. That one example of adversity in my life gave me the opportunity to grow and learn from my mistakes of being careless and ungrateful. Until this day, I have no clue on who stole my grandfather's money.

However I appreciate the lesson I learned from it. Here's what I want you to know, whatever adversity you have faced, are facing now, or about to face will be for your own good. There's beauty in the struggle and there is no such thing as a clear path to success. The road to success will have its lumps, detours, pot-holes which are all there to try to prevent you from achieving your goals. One of the steps into greatness is to not define your struggles as who you are, but to grow from them.

The reason why I am now able to tell my story is because I know that my past does not define who I am today. Once you recognize that your struggle is just one part of your testimony, you too will become invincible.

LEARN TO DISCIPLINE YOUR DISAPPOINTMENTS

If you haven't noticed by now I refer to Jim Rohn a lot in this book . His wisdom and knowledge has truly helped change my perspective about life. One of my favorite mantras from Mr. Rohn is to learn how to "Discipline your disappointments". The title of this chapter is called " Situation-ships" for a reason. I wanted to cover both situations and relation- ships because they are part of the ingredients to your recipe for success. Learning to discipline your disappointment is a skill that will save you so much from headaches and heartaches. There will be situations where you will be disappointed and people will let you down. People won't show up to support you, it'll rain the day you have your grand opening, deadlines and promises won't get met, etc. In those instance, if you aren't careful, how you react to disappointments will tear you out the game. Do not let those instances discourage you or stop you from stepping into the true and successful you. You will always be disappointed if you think that everyone has the same intent as you or your best interest at heart. We can not change people or situations, but we can change ourselves. Besides you don't want to spend time trying to change people because it will take away and distract you from committing to your purpose. My best advice to you is to keep going even through the hurt and disappointments. Seek therapy, pray, or talk to a trusted friend. The pain that you will experience during disappointment will be temporary and soon will subside. If you dwell on it, however, it can cause you to become bitter and sad-nothing will come out of feeling that way except become unproductive.

HERE ARE THREE THINGS I SUGGEST TO AVOID DISAPPOINTMENTS:

1. **Don't Think About It Too Much**. Sometimes things are just the way they are and you have to accept it just as that.

2. **Look At Things From Both Perspectives**. Don't as-sume the worst or assume the best, the wise thing to do when you face disappointment is to prepare for the worst and ex-pect the best.

3. **Stay Positive No Matter What**. Remember, never miss your opportunity to grow. Remaining positive in a situation or relationship will be beneficial in the long run.

4. **Forgive**. Forgiveness leads to freedom. Once you forgive something or someone that has disappointed you, you release it from causing you hurt and heartache. Let it go. Better days and people will enter your life, especially on your way to success. Be mindful that your transformation is like shedding layers; you have to release in order to receive. Forgiveness will only help you grow, learn and set you free.

RELATIONSHIPS: MAKE SURE THE PEOPLE YOU END UP WITH ARE ABLE TO PUT UP WITH YOU, AND BRING OUT THE BEST IN YOU.

THE WINNERS CIRCLE

Having the right people on your team will take you further than you just alone. The knowledge, resources and support you get when you surround yourself around winners has no price point. I read a book by Sophia Nelson called, "*The Woman Code*", and one of the things that she talks about in her book is knowing who is in your "front row". Knowing who and where you are seeking advice and knowledge from can help the journey become easier for you. Besides, why take advice or constructive criticism from those who have not constructed anything? Start networking, connecting and building relationships with people who've already achieved greatness and cut off toxic relationships that could be deadly to your success. You have to be okay with losing friends and people telling you how much you've changed. If you are not hearing those things from people who have not realized their own greatness, then I would worry. Still love these types of people- but from afar. As I mentioned before, your vision for yourself has to correlate to all areas in your life- including relationships.

Let me end this chapter by concluding that Life is ten percent of what happens to you and ninety percent of how you react to it. You can't change the way life is set up. Life is life and comes with ups and downs. Although you can't change life set up, and all that comes with it, the wise thing to do is to learn how life works. You may not agree on what's going on in the world, or on a lot of things. However, as visitors here on earth, the important thing is to learn the game of life and make it work according to you. Life happens to all of us. But, it's what we do with what life has given us. That's how you are able to discipline your disappointments. Every day you have two choices-to win or to lose!

I remember attending a conference in Tampa, Florida in January of 2015. The conference featured keynote speaker, Eric Thomas, who is a world renowned motivational speaker and success coach. At the conference, he quoted a story in his speech that I believe best describes how to grind and work your way out of your circumstances. It reads: *"Every morning in Africa, a gazelle wakes up, it knows it must outrun the fastest lion or it will be killed. Every morning in Africa, a lion wakes up. It knows it must run faster than the slowest gazelle, or it will starve. It doesn't matter whether you're the lion or a gazelle- when the sun comes up, you'd better be running."*

Now the question is, which one are you? Are you the lion or the gazelle in your life? In most cases, people are lions disguised as gazelles. People know that they have potential and greatness within them, however they choose to operate in fear instead of faith. If you want set a better sail this year than last year, work for it. If you want set a better sail this year than last year, work for it. If you want to live a better life, start grinding. Be the lion in your life because you can't run from what life will bring. The only way to win is to run towards life by achieving your goals. Are you ready?

In summary, we all have been in or has gone through a "situation-ship". Whether it be relationships or situations, we have to make a decision to fix or adjust both areas in our lives- especially if we feel like they are not helping us grow into our greatness. If you want to know why not you, re-evaluate what's going on in your life and begin to rebuild from where you are. Life will tear you down only to build you up and this is to make you better, wiser, and stronger. Don't let life circumstances stop you from moving forward. The goal is to learn from those experiences and to become better prepared for the next "situation-ship" that may come into your life. Remember, you were born to win. Believe and internalize it, so that the next time instead of you asking life, "Why me?" you are replacing that question with "Try me".

"IF IT'S TO BE IT IS UP TO ME"

●●●

William H Johnsen

Chapter Eleven: So Again, Why Not Me?

I am super excited about your future success story! Over the last ten chapters, I've given to you all that I have to share, to ensure that you have a great head start to your success! I want to close out this book by giving you some final tips that will help you transition you into greatness. I want you to claim success like it's your birth right- because it is after all. The only caveat to achieving the type of success you want in your life is that your work ethic has to match your dreams. If you can understand agree to those terms, and work hard towards your dreams, then you are well on your way!

Jim Rohn said it best, "Success is not what you get, it's who you become." If you want to have more, simply you have to become more. The tangible and materialistic things that comes with success are just a bi product of who you become. The feeling that comes with stepping into your own greatness is far more rewarding than the materialistic things. When your actions can finally answer the question, "So, why not me?" you have, at that moment, reached a high point in your journey. It is who you are that has true value and not the things you receive. If you want to see change in your life, guess what? You have to change, and then everything changes for you.

If you are looking to upgrade your life, then you must be willing to upgrade your thinking; whatever a man thinks he will soon become. Success is what you attract by becoming an attractive person. Your personality, attitude and mind-set are all mag- nets that draws value to your life. Let's talk about lottery winners to better explain this concept. The people who've won the lottery, then go broke within the next five years of obtaining their riches always use to puzzle me. I would always wonder how someone could lose all of that money so quickly, so I researched it! Nearly 44% of lottery winners go broke within five years because their mentality is not equipped to handle and maintain those riches- so they lose them. How can someone handle a million dollars if they are bad at maintaining what the money that they have? More money will not solve the issue if someone has a poor mindset. The skills needed for that amount of income can only be obtained if you work on you. If you give a poor man one million dollars, he will become poor again be- cause he is poor internally- his thinking is poor. A man who is wealthy on the inside can go broke and get wealthy again because he has the mindset and skills needed to get himself back on his feet. Are you getting this? If you are at that point in your life where you are saying to yourself, "So, why not me?", it is because you are now aware that something has to give in order for you to step into your own greatness… and it starts with you!

That type of transition will only go happen once you are ready to work on you. Don't worry about the money and materialistic things for now. Keep building and working on yourself, so when the materialistic things do come, you are able to sustain and keep what you've worked for.

CREATING A LEGACY

Success will be meaningless if it ends with you. If you truly want to become great, you must create something that will outlive you- something that will last forever. Your life is precious and rare and it would be sad to have settled for mediocrity. Once you've stepped into your very own greatness, it's time to help other people achieve theirs. Service and helping others are the rent we pay to live here on earth, so how will you make your deposits? Is it through making women feel beautiful through cosmetology? Will it be by teaching children how to become excellent adults? Whatever way you choose to leave your legacy, make sure you do it and lives are changed.

Do it with passion, or don't do it at all. Ask yourself, are you living to be noticed or are you trying to be remembered? That does not mean that you have to be the next Mother Theresa or Gandhi of the world- but perhaps you can embody some of their values and philosophies and be that way for your community, family or friends. Why can't you be and do just that? You can create a legacy with what you have and still be impactful if you choose to. It's all up to you and it all has to do with getting started now. Build. Create. Connect. Inspire. Do these things so that the generations to come have something to stand for and look forward to. As Maya Angelou said, "I come as one, but I stand as ten thousand". When people look at you they should be looking at the future and generations that will come after you. People should be able to see you and say, "Wow, that person's spirit and energy gives me hope for the future", or something similar to that.

How would you like to be remembered? What would you like people to say about you in your obituary? All of things has to do with what you are doing right now. The legacy starts with you –work on becoming the best you can be so that you can spend you last days in peace as opposed to resentment.

GET READY, GET SET. WIN!

I believe I have shared with you the strategies, lessons and information needed to prepare you for your new and exciting future! I am super excited about your transformation! This book is designed strategically to go over the blue print of your journey and life ahead. No matter what path you decide to take, the choice is totally up to you. I encourage you, however to take the road that has success at the end of it. Anything and everything you ever wanted is there and available to you if you simply believe and receive it to be true. The moment you realize that you can, you become awakened to your truest self. Think of right now as the first chapter to a new beginning for you – the rest of the chapters are blank pages that are waiting for you to create and design your life. I want you now to use your notes from this book and become the author of your very own destiny. It's now time to utilize and put all the information I've gathered with you, to practice it and apply it where it needs to be. Remember, whatever you do not use, ultimately you will lose, so finish this book with the eyes of a winner! From this point forward, allow success to be on your brain and courage to pour into your heart. Understand that there will be obstacles along the way, pushing you to quit and give up.

However, always have in mind of what's your purpose for wanting to become a better you. Remind yourself of what your purpose is and your "why" behind your purpose- this will help motivate you through the good times and not so good times. I want you to say this affirmation before you start game planning your next 30 days: "If it is to be, it's up to me". Say those words every morning before going out and chasing your d r e a m s . There should be no excuse after reading this book to why you do not have at least the blueprint to your new journey. Whenever you feel stuck, make an accomplishment, or just need to reflect-use this book. This book can be super useful if you make it useful. With all of that being said, congrats to your future success! Your best days start now! Let's get started!

CREATING A 30 DAY GAME PLAN

It takes 21 days to build a habit. In a month, you will not only have the skills to achieve your goals, but it will cultivate new habits that will add value to who you are and are working towards becoming. Write down three goals you have for yourself this month. Then, gradually go back to these notes and record your progress every time you get a goal accomplished. Once you start seeing results with this exercise, get in the habit of setting small monthly goals. Those goals can be drinking 5-8 glasses of water every day, leaving out the house one hour earlier to beat traffic, or to develop a business plan. Whatever your goals are, make sure that they are realistic, attainable and true to you!

30 DAY COMMITMENT CHALLENGE

Please Finish The Sentences Below

1. The resources I will need to ensure that I achieve my goals are:

____

____

____

2. I want to achieve my goals this month because:

____

____

____

3. The actions steps needed to make sure I achieve my goals are:

____

____

____

Now that you have written down your goals down, I want you to take the necessary steps to make it happen, and at the end of the month go back into these notes and reflect on your progress. I'm rooting for you!

10 COMMANDMENTS OF A WINNER

1. Thou shalt not quit on thine dreams.
2. Thou shalt work hard and give thine dreams all that I've got everyday.
3. Thou shalt not make excuses.
4. Thou shalt allow visions and dreams to be bigger than the fears
5. Thou shalt not doubt thyself, but be confident and know that success in thine future
6. Thou shalt work on thineself harder than any other area of my life.
7. Thou shalt surround thyself who holds me accountable and supports me in my dreams.
8. Thou shalt cut off toxic and unhealthy relationships.
9. Thou shalt lead from within, recognize my worth and invest in thineself.
10. Thou shalt be a game changer and help others win.

SOURCES

Chapter One: So Why Am I Here?

1. Top 10 New Year's resolutions for 2015: http://www.statisticbrain.com/new-years-resolution-statistics/
2. "Discovering Your God-Given Purpose " By Shana Schulte https://www.focusonthefamily.com/faith/faith-in-life/discovering- your-god-given-purpose/discovering-your-god-given-purpose
3. "Making the Shift Your 1st 7 Days Developing the Entrepreneur Mindset" Darren Hardy (Audio) Chapter Three: Visualize Success
1." What is a Vision Board?" http://makeavisionboard.com/what-is-a-vision-board/ess:

Chapter Four: Mindset Makeover

1. "Understanding Your Subconscious Mind" By Brian Tracy http://www.briantracy.com/blog/general/understanding-your- subconscious-mind/
2. "Energy" https://www.google.com/?gws_rd=ssl#q=energy+definition
3. Law of Attraction: The Law of Attraction Tips & Techniques That Will Blow Your Mind Away Posted on January 9, 2015 Written by Zdravko Lukovski http://enlightenmentportal.com/lawofattraction/the-law-of- attraction-tips-techniques/

Chapter Five: Internal Battle: Who's Side Are You On

1. "What to say when you talk to yourself" Book by Shad Helm Stetter Published 1986
2. Wikipedia, save "Loss Aversion": https://en.wikipedia.org/wiki/Loss_aversion
3. Michael Jordan's Biography: https://michaeljordansworld.com/acheivements.htm

Chapter Six: Creating A New You:

1. You Are a Badass: How to Stop Doubting Your Greatness and Start Living an Awesome Life by Jen Sincero Published by Running Press on April 23, 2013

Chapter Seven: Take Action...Like Now!

1. "How to Take More Action: 9 Powerful Tips "by Henrik Edberg http://www.positivityblog.com/index.php/2008/03/19/how-to- take-more-action-9-powerful-tips/
2. Colonel Harland Sanders Biography http://www.biography.com/people/colonel-harland-sanders- 12353545#kentucky-fried-chicken-is-born
3. "7 ways to grow the action habit" By Editor In Chief, PICK THE BRAIN Posted August 22, 2007 http://www.pickthebrain.com/blog/grow-the-action-habit/

Chapter Eight: The F Word(s)

1. 33 Powerful Ways of Overcoming Fear … Right Now http://www.wakeupcloud.com/overcoming-fear/

Chapter Nine: Haters? We All Have Them

1. Genesis 4 New International Version (NIV)

Chapter Ten: "Situation-ships"

1. Building Your Network Marketing Business Audio CD – 2006 by Jim Rohn

Chapter Eleven: So Again, Why Not Me

1." Why So Many Lottery Winners Go Broke" COMMENTARY by Ric Edelman January 15, 2016, 3:26 PM EST http://fortune.com/2016/01/15/powerball-lottery-winners/
2. Jim Rohn: "Jim Rohn: Success Is Something You Attract By The Person You Become" Uploaded on YouTube. Published on Aug 24, 2014
3. To Get Jim Rohn's Books: http://amzn.to/1o189m1
4. Jim Rohn: Best Life Ever: http://youtu.be/Luxgi5JZQ0c